Additive
Alert

Additive Alert

A Guide to Food Additives for the Canadian Consumer

Revised and Expanded Edition

LINDA R. PIM

Illustrated by Iain Baines

A Project of
the Pollution Probe Foundation

1981
Doubleday Canada Limited
Toronto, Ontario
Doubleday & Company, Inc.
Garden City, New York

ISBN 0-385-17714-3
Library of Congress Catalog Card Number 78-22798

Appendix D first appeared in a similar form in the March/
April 1981 and May/June 1981 issues of the *Probe Post*.

Disclaimer: Throughout this book food products are listed by
their brand names to serve as examples of food containing or
omitting various processing additives. It should be noted that
other brands of the same or similar products may have
equally positive or negative features.

For Leah and Emma

Preface to the Revised Edition

In February 1980, a headline in the magazine *Chemical Week* announced that "Food Additives Market Will Double in 1980s." The ensuing article explained that "despite agitation by some consumer advocates to have food additives eliminated, the industry continues strong. Just-completed market studies predict growth as high as 9 percent per year during the decade.... Reasons for the growth: the continued trend toward convenience foods and the extending of food shelf-life."

The two years since *Additive Alert* was first published have shown me that consumers are increasingly interested in extending their *own* shelf-lives, and are finding convenience foods to be not so convenient when account is taken of potential health effects of some of the additives therein.

As consumers, we must exert pressure on both food processors and government agencies if we feel strongly that the overall use of food additives should be moderated; that those additives of questionable safety be withdrawn from use; and that food labels should tell us more precisely what is in our food. Armed with up-to-date information, concerned individuals *can* have an impact on decisions being made about chemicals in the food supply.

This revised *Additive Alert* goes hand in hand with Pollution Probe's guide to environmental contaminants in food, *The Invisible Additives*. The former reviews the deliberately added processing chemicals that jump out at us from food labels (including colours, flavours, preservatives and thickeners). The latter examines the unintentional appearance in food of substances from the chemical sea around us (pesticides, drugs, moulds, lead, PCBs, dioxin and so on). *Additive Alert* and *The Invisible Additives* are meant to complement each other as current deposits in the consumer information bank on food chemicals.

Additive Alert has been revised in order to include new information and to report activities on the additive scene in Canada since 1979. The Guide to Suspicious Food Additives (Chapter 3) and the Food Additive Index have changed to reflect current knowledge; the Information Source List (Chapter 7) and Synopsis of Other Food Issues (now Appendix F) have been expanded; and three new appendices have been added: A Food Additive Opinion Survey (Appendix C), Twenty Most-Asked Questions About Food Additives and Some Answers (Appendix D), and Labelling Foods 'Natural': Sense and Nonsense (Appendix E).

By way of acknowledgement, I express thanks to the following individuals for their help in preparing the first edition of *Additive Alert*: Stephanie Charron and Deborah Smith (Health Protection Branch, Ontario Region, Health and Welfare Canada), Dr. Ross Hume Hall (Department of Biochemistry, McMaster University, Hamilton, Ontario), Ellen Roseman (*The Globe and Mail*), and Dr. V. Rao (Faculty of Medicine, University of Toronto); Jennifer Penney, Helen Hansen, Sheila Hulford, Peggy Schneider, Susan Crammond, Carolyn Pim and Nancy Nares (Pollution Probe volunteers); and Anne Wordsworth, Monte Hummel, Marjory Loveys and Larry Solomon (Pollution Probe staff).

The following people have been helpful in providing input to the revised edition: Adele Hurley, Nora Pim, Reva Lawry, Dr. Elizabeth Bright-See (Faculty of Medicine, University of Toronto), Barbara Davis (public health nutritionist, York Region, Ontario), Stephanie Charron, Dr. V. Rao, Dr. A.B. Morrison (Assistant Deputy Minister, Health Protection Branch, Health and Welfare Canada), Kathleen Francoeur-Hendriks (Assistant Deputy Minister, Consumer Affairs, Consumer and Corporate Affairs Canada) and Andrew Roman (Public Interest Advocacy Centre). Finally, thanks go out to all the friendly, hard-working people at Doubleday Canada, including Rick Archbold and Janet Turnbull (editors) and Carolynne Hastings (publicity manager).

LINDA R. PIM
May 1981

Contents

Why this book?

One hundred percent of Canadians eat for a living. But not all 100% are aware of just what they are eating. Many of us would like to understand the long list of ingredients on the side of the cookie package. We would also like to know why the list is so long. Yet there has been no thorough publication available on the subject of food additives that addresses a Canadian audience. This book is intended to fill that need.

How to use it

This book is a *hand*book. It outlines the types of food additives (Chapter Two); indicates which specific additives may be unsafe (Chapter Three); unravels the complex web of food additive laws in Canada (Chapter Four); and suggests what you can do about the proliferation of additives in our food (Chapters Five and Six).

Carry this handbook with you when you shop for food. Use the index of all food additives in Canada (at the back of the book) to avoid the worst additives and to be aware of what the others are. Compare brands to determine whether one is freer of additives than another. Make an informed choice. If you don't like the choice, let it be known—to the food processor, the supermarket, the federal Health Protection Branch, your Member of Parliament. Do it!

ONE

"We Are What We Eat. So Why Should I Eat Butylated Hydroxyanisole?"

Good question! Your body wouldn't last long without phenylalanine (a protein component), linoleic acid (a fat component) or calciferol (Vitamin D), but it will do quite nicely without butylated hydroxyanisole (BHA, a food preservative). Whether or not the modern food distribution system requires the use of BHA is another question.

Let's begin with a game. Try to guess what these everyday foods are, on the basis of the ingredients listed on the package label:

sugar (may also contain dextrose), modified cornstarch, salt, mono- and diglycerides, sodium phosphate, artificial and natural flavour, food colour, maltol, citric acid, tricalcium phosphate

(Answer: Jell-O Vanilla Instant Pudding)

enriched white flour (thiamine mononitrate, riboflavin, niacin and reduced iron), glucose-fructose or glucose and/or sugar, whey and/or whey powder, yeast, lard and/or vegetable oil,

"I feel so worthless. I'm all food additives, food colours, texture agents. I've no real food value at all."

shortening, salt, calcium propionate, calcium sulfate, ammonium chloride, potassium bromate, ascorbic acid, L-cysteine (hydrochloride), mono and diglycerides, sodium stearoyl-2-lactylate

(Answer: Sliced Upper Crust Enriched White Bread)

sugar (may also contain dextrose), corn dextrin, cellulose gum, citric acid, tricalcium phosphate, xanthan gum, natural orange flavour, artificial flavour, food colour, vitamin C (214 mg per 100 g)

(Answer: Tang Orange Breakfast Crystals)

These lists of ingredients read like the index of a chemistry textbook! Compare with the following:

milk, eggs, cornstarch, fruit juice, sugar

(Answer: a home-made pudding)

whole wheat flour, water, cracked wheat, brown sugar, honey, shortening, wheat gluten, yeast, sea salt, wheat germ, soya flour. (Refrigerate after opening.)

(Answer: Dempster's Whole Earth Bread)

pure, frozen, concentrated orange juice

(Answer: What else?!)

Health and Welfare Canada estimates that we eat six to seven pounds of food additives per person each year.

About three-quarters of the food consumed in North America undergoes some sort of chemical alteration between the time it leaves the farm gate and the time it appears on the dinner table. It has not always been this way. In the film *Eat, Drink and Be Wary*, nutritionist Jean Mayer speaks of the conversion of our western food system from one that was primarily agricultural to one that is primarily industrial. Most of this transformation has taken place since the end of World War Two and parallels industrialization and growth in other sectors of the economy of Canada and other countries, such as the proliferation of consumer goods.

As the label game illustrates, what may seem like simple foods—a pudding, a loaf of bread, an orange drink—can be altered to produce items similar in form but different in content. The features of these industrialized foods are made possible because of the use of *food additives*. They allow the orange drink crystals to remain fresh in the kitchen cupboard for months on end; make the enriched white bread light and spongy and prevent the development of mould, and promote the essential texture in the (egg-less) packaged pudding. Viewed another way, food additives may either modify a familiar food (the bread example) or create an entirely new food (the fabricated orange drink example).

We can look at food additives in two broad categories. First there are those which prevent food from "going bad" (by inhibiting the formation of moulds, the activity of bacteria and the development of rancidity). Second there are those which make food more appealing, be it in colour, flavour or texture. The North American food-processing system often finds itself sacrificing the natural attributes of food (such as its own inherent colour and flavour) in favour of industrially suitable qualities such as uniformity of composition, suitability to manufacturing procedures and long "shelf life" (the period over which a food product remains fresh and available for sale). What is taken out of a "natural" (unprocessed) food usually ends up going back in, albeit in a different form. For example, many vegetable oils contain tocopherol (or Vitamin E) and carotenoids (related to Vitamin A) which help prevent the oil from becoming rancid. Factory processing destroys these compounds, so a synthetic antioxidant preservative such as butylated hydroxyanisole (BHA) must be added instead.

Or must it? We should be careful to distinguish among different uses for food additives. Some uses really are utilitarian (such as the addition of preservatives when refrigeration is not available). On the other hand, some uses serve only as unduly precautionary measures (such as adding BHA to vegetable oil in the highly unlikely event that it may require a preservative) or have only "cosmetic" or esthetic effects (such as adding artificial colour to orange skins).

Let's look at some of the prevailing myths on the food additive front:

● *All additives are 'badditives.'*
To argue that all additives are harmful is as absurd as to say that they are all safe.

● *Life is just a bowl of chemicals, so there's no harm in adding a few more. Besides, lots of unprocessed foods have harmful chemicals in them.*
Why should we add more hazards to the ones we already face (poison mushrooms, toxic rhubarb leaves and cyanide in apple seeds, to name three)?

● *We need food additives to increase the world food supply. They will solve the world food crisis!*
Counterfeit chocolate and frosted pop tarts will *not* feed the hungry planet. Food additives are used almost exclusively to alter the food supply of the world's industrialized countries, not the underdeveloped and undernourished ones.

● *The small amounts of food additives permitted in food won't hurt you.*

Neither will one cigarette or one alcoholic beverage. Of significance here is possible harm from low doses of food additives consumed daily over the course of a lifetime.

● *Let's remember that much of the processing of the food we eat goes on right in our own kitchens.*

Home processing—chopping, mixing, boiling, baking—is of quite a different nature from factory processing: emulsifying, refining, extracting, preserving, colouring, flavouring.

● *Our supermarket food prices would skyrocket if it weren't for additives.*

This might be true with respect to avoiding possible spoilage through some uses of preservatives (for example, in unrefrigerated bread), but there's no reason that taking the colour out of Kraft Cracker Barrel Cheddar Cheese should raise its price.

TWO

An Eater's Digest of Food Additives in Canada

Let's begin the digest with the definition of "food additive" according to Canadian law:

"Food additive" means any substance, including any source of radiation, the use of which results, or may reasonably be expected to result in it or its byproducts becoming a part of or affecting the characteristics of a food, *but does not include* [my italics]:

(a) any nutritive material that is used, recognized, or commonly sold as an article or ingredient of food,

(b) vitamins, mineral nutrients and amino acids,

(c) spices, seasonings, flavouring preparations, essential oils, oleoresins and natural extractives,

(d) agricultural chemicals

(e) food packaging materials and components thereof, and

(f) drugs recommended for administration to animals that may be consumed as food

7

This is section B.01.001 of the *Food and Drug Regulations*. All the above exclusions are treated elsewhere in the *Regulations* with varying degrees of thoroughness.

One might be tempted to define a food additive more simply as "anything listed on a food label that doesn't sound familiar." The reason that additives do not sound "familiar" is because very few of them have common names. In a kitchen cupboard may be found such items as sodium chloride, acetic acid, sucrose and sodium bicarbonate, but they sound more familiar if we use their common names—salt, vinegar, sugar and baking soda.

Some avid proponents of the widespread use of food additives point to the fact that ordinary salt and sugar are the most commonly and abundantly

used additives. These two will not be treated as additives in this handbook because, although they can both serve as preservatives, the preserving effect is achieved only at relatively high concentrations of salt or sugar (such as in jams and jellies, with respect to sugar, and in salt pork, with respect to salt). Sugar and salt are more often thought of as ingredients characteristic of the food rather than as additives *per se*. (Federal food regulations do not include sugar and salt as food additives.) Both are suspected of contributing to the development or aggravation of several diseases—for example, adult-onset diabetes, with respect to sugar, and cardiovascular disease, with respect to salt.

Vitamins, minerals and other nutrient supplements are likewise not included as additives in this handbook, since their chief purpose is to improve the nutritional quality of the food; additives are not used with this aim foremost in mind. However, because these nutrient supplements are often listed by their chemical names on food labels, they are included (in parentheses) in "The Food Additive Index" at the end of the handbook.

The index lists each additive permitted in food sold in Canada, states what kind of additive it is (colour, preservative, emulsifying agent, and so on) and indicates, in bold type, which additives are suspect in terms of safety.

In this chapter, we describe the different classes of food additives to find out what purposes they are supposed to serve in our food, give a few examples of additives in each class, and list some foods in which you will find these additives. In the next

chapter, we'll look at the safety question and single
out those additives of questionable merit.

Colours

Colouring compounds are added to food primarily
to give it an appetizing appearance, on the strength
of the notion that the way a food looks has an effect
on palatability, or how good someone thinks it
tastes. Most people have become so accustomed to
the standard colour of a food product that many
would not accept the product if the colour were
substantially changed. Would you eat blue butter?!
On the other hand, what's wrong with white margarine, or mottled orange-green orange skins, or
pale yellow cheddar cheese, or . . . ?

Food processors often add colours to their products to restore original colour present in the fresh
produce which has been lost in processing—for example, green colour in pickles. In the case of completely artificial or "fabricated" foods, colours are
added to simulate the attributes of "the real thing"
—for example, orange colour in orange drink flavour crystals. Sometimes colour is added to give the
illusion of a highly nutritious product. For example,
yellow colour is added to some bakery products to
make them appear to be rich in eggs, and brown
colour is added to some bread so that it is darker
and supposedly more of a "whole grain" bread than
it really is. (However, bread in Canada must contain at least 60% whole wheat flour to qualify as
"whole wheat bread," regardless of added colour.)

Most of the colours used in food today are synthetic dyes. Since they have strong colouring power, only a small amount is needed to achieve the desired result in a food product. Although thirty-three different colouring agents are approved for use in Canadian food, you won't find them listed on food labels. The law states that only the word "colour" must appear on a label. (We'll explore this legal loop-hole, and many others, later on.)

Colours serve no utilitarian purpose in our food and are added solely for cosmetic reasons. Every effort should be made to remove them as soon as possible, if only because they are of no real benefit to the consumer.

Some common food colours are:
    amaranth
    annatto
    caramel
    tartrazine
    citrus red no. 2

Some foods which contain food colour are:
    Fleischmann's Margarine
    McCormick's Some of Each Party Crackers
    Jell-O Lemon Jelly Powder
    Cool Whip Dessert Topping
    Kraft Singles Process Cheese Slices
    Ingersoll Cheese Spread
    Aylmer Fruit Cocktail
    Aunt Jemima Pancake Syrup
    Peek Freans Assorted Biscuits
    Bick's Sweet Gherkins
    Maple Leaf Creamery Butter

Preservatives

The World Health Organization estimates that about 20% of the world food supply is lost due to spoilage. Since it is impossible for most of us, especially in the industrialized countries, to live directly off the land year round, some method of food preservation is necessary. Addition of chemical preservatives to food is only one means of preventing or retarding spoilage. Other more common methods of food preservation include drying, freezing (for example, pre-mixed and pre-kneaded frozen dough usually contains no preservatives), refrigerating, salting, sweetening, curing, spicing, pickling, and fermenting. If none of these methods were available, the food supply would be in serious jeopardy.

In cases where no other means of preservation is suitable and where, indeed, some form of preservation is essential, chemical preservatives which have been proven safe have a definite role to play. But we must take note of instances where preservatives are used more for the benefit of the food processor than the consumer. If the processor has the opportunity to get a "deal" on a large batch of an ingredient for one of its food products, chances are the ingredient will sit around the factory for some time and hence will require some means of preservation. If the ingredients are always fresh, then preservatives could often be eliminated. Or a preservative may be used to extend the shelf life of a product, when other procedures could eliminate the need for the chemical (see box).

In some cases, it may be true that if preservatives

In a letter of December 1977, Edward
Pasquale, Jr., President of Unico Foods
Limited of Toronto, writes:

"We feel that preservatives are not needed in
our vegetable oils for a number of reasons:
1. We package fresh oil daily at our Toronto
   plant.... We employ highly qualified
   quality control personnel at our plant...
   and we take every precaution to ensure that
   the oil is of the finest quality before we
   pack.
2. We have a very high turn-over. Once the
   oils are packed, they are sold very quickly.
3. Usually, we never carry in our warehouse
   any oils that are more than two weeks old.
4. We make every effort to control the
   rotation of oils at the store level also,
   through our own sales staff.
5. Consumer complaints about rancid oil are
   almost non-existent.... Many of our
   customers do seem to prefer an oil without
   preservatives."

were not used, food costs would rise because of
waste from spoilage. Much depends on how close
the consumer is, in time and space, to the source of
food supply: the closer the two are, the less critical
the addition of preservatives. The butylated hydroxyanisole present in Tenderflake Pure Lard would
probably never fulfill its preservative function when
sold in Toronto where it is produced, but it might

just fill the bill for a variety store in a summer resort area where goods sit on the shelf for a much longer period before being sold. In other words, our food processing industries are centralized in large towns and cities to the extent that, although preserving chemicals are likely not required for many shipments, they are necessary for markets further from the point of production.

Thus one way to cut down on preservative use would be to decentralize food processing. At the consumer level, the need for preservatives could be reduced or eliminated through more frequent purchases of smaller quantities of food. Taking bread as an example, the options are either to maintain the current, centralized bakery system which relies heavily on preservatives, or to revert to the European practice of frequent bread purchases from local bakeries.

Some common preservatives and foods which contain them are:

>*sodium nitrite*—Maple Leaf Bacon, Schneider's Cooked Ham, Maple Leaf Summer Sausage
>
>*sodium nitrate*—Kraft Gouda Cheese (Product of Holland)
>
>*butylated hydroxyanisole* (BHA) and/or *butylated hydroxytoluene* (BHT)—Kellogg's Corn Flakes, Kellogg's Raisin Bran, Nabisco Shredded Wheat,* Carnation Scalloped Potatoes, Tenderflake Pure Lard, Crisco Vegetable Oil
>
>*potassium metabisulphite*—Sunkist Reconstituted Lemon Juice

* BHA and/or BHT are usually added to the cereal packaging material rather than to the cereal itself; the preservative slowly migrates into the food.

sulphur dioxide (also an air pollutant)—Sun-Maid Golden Seedless Raisins
potassium sorbate—McNair Large Prunes
sodium benzoate—Blue Bonnet Margarine
calcium propionate—Dominion 100% Whole Wheat Bread
monoisopropyl citrate—Mazola Corn Oil

Flavours

Natural and artificial flavours are the most numerous of the food additives—they number as many as 1,500, or about three times the number of all the other permitted additives combined. Since World War Two, the use of flavourings has grown tremendously, in step with the development of "fabricated" foods and new methods of food distribution. Simulated (artificial) flavourings are a very important class of food additives since they can replace "the real thing," an expensive natural product that is often in short supply. A prime example is artificial vanilla flavour ("vanillin"), which replaces the real extract of vanilla beans. If a food contains artificial flavour, one can usually assume that any natural flavour listed on the label is there in a token amount so that it may be listed (see box). Incredible as it may seem, Canada has very few restrictions on the use of flavours in our food. A food label won't tell you much since only the words "artificial flavour" or "natural flavour" are required. Some foods which you wouldn't expect to contain added flavours do. For example:

Fry's Pure Cocoa

> "'Bee-Rich' is an imitation honey that comes in tank car lots from the Rich-Federal Company of Buffalo, New York. According to the product data sheet, 'Bee-Rich' is an imitation honey that has all the characteristics of pure honey; such as *flavour* [italics mine], bouquet, humectant properties, high yeast stability and labelling advantages. What are those labelling advantages? Because it contains some real honey, 'Bee-Rich' is a valuable sales tool for the end user through the use of honey in label declaration . . . The food companies add a little bit of the genuine stuff so that they can put it on the list."
>
> ROSS HUME HALL, *Canadian Consumer,*
> October 1976.

Peek Freans Digestive Biscuits
Becker's Buttermilk
Sealtest Light 'n' Lively Peach Yogurt
Maple Leaf Bacon (smoke flavour!)

Flavour Enhancers

Flavour enhancers would more aptly be called "potentiators" because they increase the potency of food flavour without themselves contributing to flavour *per se*. Ordinary table salt can act as a flavour enhancer at concentrations so low that the salty flavour is undetectable. But salt is a relative weakling compared with the newer breed of flavour enhancers, primarily the kingpin, monosodium glutamate (MSG). Notes U.S. food additives writer Beatrice Trum Hunter: "MSG is much used to step up the indifferent or undistinguished flavor of many canned and processed foods." Flavour enhancers must be listed on Canadian food labels, but there are no restrictions on where and at what levels they're used.

Some common flavour enhancers and foods which contain them are:

> *monosodium glutamate* — Campbell's Soups (Cream of Mushroom, Vegetable Beef, Bean with Bacon, Cheddar Cheese, etc.), Bovril Chicken Bouillon Instant Mix, Lawry's Seasoned Salt, Lipton Country Style French Style Onion Soup Mix, Hostess Onion-Flavoured Rings, Planters Dry Roasted Peanuts, Accent (pure MSG)

> *disodium inosinate* and/or *disodium guanylate* — Nestlé Souptime Chicken Vegetable Instant Soup Mix, Hostess Tortilla Chips

Texture Agents

These additives modify a food's texture in order to give it a desired consistency. They include: emulsifiers, to prevent separation of liquids, such as oil and vinegar in a salad dressing; stabilizers, to prevent settling of suspended particles, such as the chocolate in chocolate milk; gelling agents, to promote the formation of a gel, such as in gelatin desserts; thickening agents to thicken a liquid, such as corn starch in a pie filling.

Some foods could not exist without texture agents. Who ever heard of drinking a bowl of Jell-

O? On the other hand, some texture agents are added only for the sake of convenience—who would want to take the energy to shake a bottle of salad dressing to mix the oil and vinegar anyway?! Or, they may be added to imitate what should be a natural texture. Yoghurt so thick you could stand a spoon in it can be produced without gelatin; it is, however, a more delicate process that does not disturb the bacterial culture necessary in yoghurt production.

Some common texture agents and foods which contain them are:

Emulsifiers and Stabilizers

> *propylene glycol alginate*—Kraft Thousand Island Salad Dressing
>
> *polysorbate 60*—Cool Whip Dessert Topping
>
> *carrageenan*—Carnation Evaporated Milk, Sealtest "All Natural" Vanilla Ice Cream, Sealtest Sour Cream
>
> *mono- and diglycerides*—Dempster's Stone Ground 100% Whole Wheat Bread, Loblaws Margarine, Christie's Sliced Upper Crust Enriched White Bread

Gelling and Thickening Agents

> *gelatin*—Jell-O Jelly Powders, Sealtest Peach Yogurt
>
> *starch*—Jell-O Puddings and Pie Fillings, Campbell's Scotch Broth Soup

Bleaching, Maturing, and Dough Conditioning Agents

As stated in Health and Welfare Canada's *Guide to Food Additives*, "freshly milled flour has a creamy colour because it contains carotenoids, the same pigments that make certain fruits and vegetables yellow. If stored for several months, flour becomes whiter and its baking qualities improve due to oxidation. However, the natural aging process is slow and the results are not always consistent. Storage also increases the final cost of the product and the danger of deterioration and infestation from insects and rodents. Bleaching and maturing agents hasten the oxidation and aging process and result in flour of consistent quality and colour. Dough conditioners ... improve the handling properties of the dough and reduce mixing time, resulting in better texture, volume, and grain in bakery products."

Some common bleaching, maturing and dough conditioning agents and foods which contain them are:

> *benzoyl peroxide*—Loblaws All-Purpose Enriched Flour
>
> *azodicarbonamide*—Five Roses Whole Wheat Flour
>
> *sodium stearoyl-2-lactylate*—Christie Old Country Crusty Bread

Anti-Caking Agents

Certain dry food products tend to absorb moisture from the air, causing them to form clumps. If an anti-caking agent is added, caking or clumping is avoided.

The labels of many foods to which anti-caking agents may be added are not required to list the agents as such. Therefore, we can list here only some anti-caking agents and types of foods which may contain them: Calcium aluminum stearate, calcium stearate, magnesium carbonate and silicon dioxide may be found in cake mixes, icing sugar, baking powder, table salt and garlic salt.

Food Enzymes

Enzymes perform in food processing the same functions they perform in the human body: they help to initiate desired reactions. The most common food enzymes are rennet and pepsin. They are used to curdle milk in the making of most types of cheese and are listed on cheese packages.

Acid/Base Balancing Additives

Certain additives can be used to control the acid/alkali balance (or pH) in food, a characteristic that can affect cooking results, flavour, and texture. Also, acid-reacting materials are necessary in leavening agents used to produce the carbon dioxide that makes a batter bubbly and a cake light.

Some common acid/base balancing additives and foods which contain them are:

citric acid—Loblaws Stewed Tomatoes
sodium carbonate—Fry's Pure Cocoa
sodium bicarbonate—Ritz Crackers
calcium phosphate, monobasic—Magic Baking Powder

Firming Agents

These additives ensure that canned fruits and vegetables do not go soft as a result of heat treatment during processing and assist in the coagulation of milk during the production of some cheeses.

Two common firming agents and foods which contain them are:

> *calcium chloride*—Aylmer Tomatoes, A & P Old Cheddar Cheese
>
> *calcium sulphate*—Loblaws Tomatoes

Sequestering Agents

Sequestering additives combine with trace amounts of metals (such as iron and copper) in foods and inactivate them so that their undesirable effects on the colour, flavour, and texture of foods are avoided.

Two common sequestering agents and foods which contain them are:

> *calcium disodium EDTA*—Kraft Thousand Island Dressing
>
> *calcium phosphate*—Ice Castle Strawberry Ice Cream

Starch Modifying Agents

Starch is used in many foods to extend, thicken, stabilize and modify texture. (See "Texture Agents" above.) But most starch is present in food as "modified starch," modified depending on the conditions under which it is to be used. For example, "natural" corn starch will not mix properly in cold water; a chemically modified starch will. Other starch modifiers allow starch to remain stable at high temperatures, to be able to withstand rough agitation in processing machinery, and to cope with variations in acidity.

You will not find starch modifying agents listed on food labels since there is no requirement that this be done. All that will be listed is "modified starch." (All starch modifiers are of a food grade quality, with impurities removed; their other uses— also shown here—would not demand as pure a substance.)

Some common starch modifiers are:

> *hydrochloric acid* (a primary component of digestive juices in the stomach)
> *sodium hydroxide* (caustic soda)
> *hydrogen peroxide* (also used to bleach hair)
> *nitric acid* (also used in making explosives)

Yeast Foods

Yeast foods act as nutrients for the yeasts used in bakery products and some alcoholic beverages. The latter do not require ingredient lists on their labels; you must contact the brewery, winery or distillery for this information.

Two common yeast foods and foods which contain them are:

> *ammonium chloride*—Hollywood Dark Bread, Christie's Sliced Upper Crust Enriched White Bread
> *calcium sulphate*—Toastmaster Sliced Sandwich Enriched White Bread, Christie's Cracked Wheat Bread

Glazing and Polishing Agents

These additives impart a shiny surface to candy and cake decorations.

Two common glazing and polishing agents and foods which contain them are:

　　gum arabic—McCormick's Ju-Jubes
　　shellac—Cadbury Calypso Peanuts

Others include beeswax and carnauba wax.

Extraction (Carrier) Solvents

These liquids are used to isolate or extract desirable components from various foodstuffs. They are used to extract the yellow colour from annatto seeds for use in butter and margarine, the oils from peanuts and sunflower seeds, the caffeine from coffee beans (in the production of decaffeinated coffee) and flavours and colours from various sources. Residues of these solvents may remain in the food, although ideally, none should remain.

You will not find extraction solvents listed on food labels since there is no requirement that this be done.

Some common extraction solvents are:

　　ethyl alcohol (as in alcoholic beverages)
　　castor oil (a strong laxative)
　　acetone (also used in making varnishes and resins)
　　methyl alcohol ("wood alcohol," also used as a fuel; fatal in larger quantities than found in extracted products)

Miscellaneous Additives

This is a catch-all category of additives with a variety of purposes.

Anti-foaming agents are used to prevent foaming in the processing of jams and cooking oils. For example Crisco Vegetable Oil contains the anti-foaming agent dimethylpolysiloxane.

Humectants ensure that foods requiring a certain degree of moisture are prevented from drying out. For example, Dalton's Sweetened Featherflake Coconut contains the humectant sorbitol.

Pressure dispensing agents act as propellants for food packaged in aerosol cans. For example, nitrous oxide (also an air pollutant) is the propellant in Top Wip dessert topping.

Release agents prevent food from sticking to baking surfaces during manufacture. They are not required to be listed on food labels. Some common release agents are mineral oil, calcium stearate and sorbitol (also a humectant).

Whipping agents help achieve a stable whipped product. Sodium stearoyl-2-lactylate (also a dough conditioner) is an example.

Carriers for flour bleaching, maturing and dough conditioning agents include calcium carbonate (lime), calcium phosphate dibasic and tribasic, and calcium sulphate. They are not required to be listed on food labels.

Other miscellaneous food additives include *wetting agents* (for dry beverage mixes), *anti-sprouting agents* (for potatoes and onions), *plasticizing agents* (for chewing gum), *dusting agents* (also for chewing gum) and *coatings* (for fresh fruits and vegetables, and cheeses).

THREE

The Pollution Probe Guide to Suspicious Food Additives

So you think that all the food additives permitted in food sold in Canada have been proven to be safe? Don't we all wish that were the case! What would you think if you discovered that a food dye that colours about one-third of the factory-processed food in Canada is banned in the United States? Well, it's true; amaranth (U.S. red no. 2) is a Mr. Hyde in the U.S., a Dr. Jekyll in Canada. The reverse is true for allura red (U.S. red no. 40)—not permitted in Canada, but considered benign in the U.S. (Red no. 40 is currently under heavy fire in the U.S.; the Food and Drug Administration is re-examining its alleged safety. A curious twist to the Canadian situation is the fact that allura red is permitted to colour drug products but not foods.)

Remember that in general food additives, unlike the chemicals used on the farm as pesticides, are not designed to be toxic. Some preservatives may be looked upon as exceptions to this rule, since they act as fungicides (for example, in preventing mould

in bread) and bacteriocides (for example, in killing the botulism-causing bacterium *Clostridium botulinum*). Although most additives would have to be eaten in large single doses to produce immediate symptoms of toxicity, there is a broad area of doubt concerning the effects of eating small amounts of additives over the course of a lifetime.

Below are listed those food additives permitted in Canadian food which are *at least seriously suspected of having detrimental health effects on human beings.* Some have been proven harmful. In a short period of time (minutes or hours or days) we may see the acute effects of a food additive, particularly with regard to allergic reactions. (Some hyperactive children improve markedly when certain food additives are removed from their diets.) But more insidious are those effects, such as cancer, which may result from years of chronic, low-dose exposure to the chemical in question.

The International Agency for Research on Cancer (which is affiliated with the World Health Organization of the United Nations) has estimated that 80 to 90 percent of all cancers are caused by environmental factors. This does *not* mean that we always *know* which chemical or what aspect of our lifestyle is a culprit, but simply that most cancer has some sort of environmental rather than genetic (hereditary) origin. The proven link between tobacco and lung cancer is one of the few cases in which cause and effect are indisputable. Other key environmental sources of cancer include sunlight (as a cause of skin cancer), medical and dental x-rays, and occupational exposure to certain industrial chemicals. The link between food chemicals and cancer is less clear.

Still, eating is a daily, life-long activity and our food does contain a number of additives that have been linked, even if only conjecturally, with cancer. So we must look closely at diet as a source of cancer. If a chemical can be proven to cause cancer in one species of animal, scientists assume it capable of causing cancer in all life forms, including humans.

The questionable additives listed below are the ones about which there is some evidence of health effects. Many food additives, particularly those that have been permitted in Canadian food since before 1964 when food regulations took their present form, have not been tested for long-term, low-dose effects. Information about the toxicity of these additives is only slowly surfacing.

Here is the "suspect list." (With each additive are given some foods in or on which its use is permitted. This does *not* mean that all brands of a given product contain the additive. Read the label! Also given are the effects of the additive on laboratory animals.)

COLOURS

Name	Effects on test animals (and/or humans, if known)	Permitted in
amaranth (U.S. red dye no. 2)	tumour production; allergic and respiratory reactions; teratogenic effects*; linked to hyperactivity in children	jams & jellies, butter, bread, ice cream, flavoured milk, pickles, ketchup, concentrated fruit juice
erythrosine	allergic and respiratory reactions; interference with iodine metabolism; linked to hyperactivity in children	as above
indigotine	increased sensitivity to viral diseases; linked to hyperactivity in children	as above

sunset yellow FCF	allergic reactions; linked to hyperactivity in children	as above
tartrazine (U.S. yellow dye no. 5)	allergic reactions, especially in people sensitive to acetylsalicylic acid (ASA) and the benzoate preservatives; asthma; linked to hyperactivity in children	as above
brilliant blue FCF (U.S. blue dye no. 1)	tumour production; allergic reactions; linked to hyperactivity in children; FAO/WHO** recommend against its use	as above
fast green FCF	allergic reactions; tumour production	as above
citrus red no. 2	weak carcinogen†; FAO/WHO recommend against its use	orange skins only
ponceau SX (U.S. red dye no. 4)	damage to urinary system; banned in U.S.	fruit peel and maraschino cherries only
carbon black	tumour production; not permitted in U.S.	jams & jellies, concentrated fruit juice, dried egg, ice cream, bread, butter, vegetable fats & oils, margarine, cheese, icing sugar, pickles, flavoured milk, processed meat & fish

iron oxide (rust!)	unclear, although this colour has been banned in the countries of the EEC	as above
titanium dioxide	as for iron oxide	as above
cochineal	teratogenic effects	as above
caramel	neurological disorders; effects on disease immunity systems; most toxic when ammonia compounds are used in caramel production	brown bread, flavoured milk, butter, concentrated fruit juice, ice cream, sherbet, jams & jellies, pickles & relishes, alcoholic beverages

*Birth defects
**Food and Agriculture Organization and World Health Organization (affiliated with the United Nations)
†A carcinogen is a cancer-causing agent

FLAVOURS

Flavours constitute the largest class of food additives, but the class we know least about with respect to safety. "It is probably fair to say that flavours pose the largest regulatory task, not only because there are so many of them but also because of insufficient toxicological data, rapid changes in the field and many other factors. In general little is known about the toxicological aspects of flavours. ...Governments have approached the question of controlling flavours from various directions. Some publish lists of permitted and prohibited flavours; some have a short list of prohibited flavours, many of which are natural, and others allow flavourings (both natural and synthetic) that are found only in the aromatic oils of edible plants." (G. O. Kermode, *Scientific American*, March 1972. Canada has none of the restrictions mentioned.)

Many flavour additives have been linked to allergic or other hypersensitive reactions in humans, including coughing, asthma, urticaria (hives), heartburn, headaches, migraine headaches, and hyperactivity in children.

FLAVOUR ENHANCERS

Name	Effects on test animals (and/or humans, if known)	Permitted in
brominated vegetable oil	accumulation in tissues, various anatomical abnormalities	citrus- and spruce-flavoured drinks
caffeine	stimulation of nervous system; aggravation of hyperactivity in children; linked to birth defects in humans	cola drinks
monosodium glutamate (MSG)	allergic reactions ("Chinese Restaurant Syndrome"); brain damage; possible psychological effects (e.g., depression); possible birth defects	snack foods, tinned soups, much restaurant food (almost no restrictions on its use)
tannic acid	liver damage including tumours	chewing gum

disodium inosinate and disodium guanylate	safe except for people suffering from gout and other conditions requiring avoidance of purines	some snack foods (no restrictions on their use)
hydrolyzed vegetable protein	comprised largely of monosodium glutamate; see MSG (above)	not used in baby foods; no other restrictions on use
maltol	effects on blood composition	no restrictions on use

PRESERVATIVES

Name	*Effects on test animals (and/or humans, if known)*	*Permitted in*
sulphites (sodium and potassium metabisulphite, sodium and potassium bisulphite, sodium sulphite)	possible interference with metabolism of the B vitamin thiamin and other B vitamins, vitamin A and calcium; toxic interaction of sulphites and unsaturated fats; intestinal changes	cider, wine, beer, jams & jellies, molasses, marmalades, fruit juices, tomato paste, dried fruits & vegetables
nitrites (sodium and potassium nitrite)	induction of methaemoglobinemia (a blood disorder), especially in infants; tumour production in conversion of nitrites to (carcinogenic) nitrosamines; mutagenic* and teratogenic effects; allergic reactions in humans ("nitrite headache")	processed meat and preserved poultry

nitrates (sodium and potassium nitrate)	conversion to nitrites (see above)	preserved meat, some ripened cheeses
butylated hydroxytoluene (BHT)	reproductive failures; behavioural effects; blood cell changes; lung, stomach and ovarian tumours, especially in conjunction with presence of nitrosamines; possible toxic effects on humans from long-term storage in fatty tissues; linked to *decreased* risk of stomach cancer; allergic reactions in humans; possible interference with activity of ingested steroid hormones and oral contraceptives in humans	vegetable oils & shortenings, dry breakfast cereals, dry beverage mixes, chewing gum, snack foods, instant potatoes, margarine
butylated hydroxyanisole (BHA)	see BHT; fewer effects reported and less use in food than BHT	as above
propyl gallate	reproductive failures; liver damage	vegetable oils & shortenings, dry breakfast cereals, margarine, instant potatoes, snack foods, chewing gum
benzoic acid and **sodium benzoate**	neurological disorders; allergic reactions in humans, especially those sensitive to acetylsalicylic acid (ASA); asthma;	jams & jellies, mincemeat, marmalade, ketchup, marinated meat & fish, fruit juices, margarine

benzoic acid and **sodium benzoate** (continued)	synergy with the preservative sodium bisulphite	
sodium propionate	linked to migraine headaches in humans	bread, cheese
sulphur dioxide	destruction of the B vitamin thiamin	dried fruits & vegetables, beverages

*causing genetic changes

TEXTURE AGENTS

Name	*Effects on test animals (and/or humans, if known)*	*Permitted in*
carboxymethyl cellulose (and sodium carboxymethyl cellulose)	may cause intestinal obstruction; suspected carcinogen	salad dressings, flavoured milk, processed cheese, ice cream, cream, cottage cheese
carrageenan (and sodium carrageenan, calcium carrageenan)	gastrointestinal ulcers (but also used to treat ulcers in humans); liver lesions; effects on immunity system; suspected carcinogen	salad dressings, prepared meat & fish, flavoured milk, processed cheese, ice cream, evaporated milk, cream, cottage cheese, sour cream, infant formula, alcoholic beverages
modified starch (containing one or more of the 23 permitted starch modifying agents; e.g., epichlorohydrin)	epichlorohydrin: kidney damage, mutagenic effects (chromosome changes), including suspected carcinogenicity	puddings & pie fillings, gravies, sauces, baby foods

polyoxyethylene (8) stearate	effects on gastrointestinal and urinary tracts (e.g., bladder stones, tumours)	bakery foods
saponin	weight loss; effects on gestation period; blood disorders	beverage mixes, soft drinks
sodium alginate	inhibition of essential metal absorption; allergic reactions in humans	salad dressings, ice cream, flavoured milk, processed cheese
tragacanth gum	allergic reactions in humans	salad dressings, processed cheese, cream cheese, cottage cheese, ice cream, sherbet

FLOUR BLEACHING AGENTS

Name	*Effects on test animals (and/or humans, if known)*	*Permitted in*
benzoyl peroxide	destruction of vitamin E; allergic reactions; weak carcinogen	flour, whole wheat flour

ACID/BASE BALANCING ADDITIVES

Name	*Effects on test animals (and/or humans, if known)*	*Permitted in*
alum (potassium aluminum sulphate; also a firming agent and flour bleach carrier)	kidney damage, intestinal bleeding	pickles, relish, flour, baking powder, beer, ale

sodium aluminum sulphate	kidney damage	baking powder (used for other purposes in pickles & relishes, flour)

SEQUESTERING AGENTS

Name	*Effects on test animals (and/or humans, if known)*	*Permitted in*
calcium disodium EDTA	possible interference with absorption of essential trace metals such as iron, zinc and copper	salad dressings, alcoholic beverages

MISCELLANEOUS ADDITIVES

Name	*Effects on test animals (and/or humans, if known)*	*Permitted in*
silicates (magnesium silicate, magnesium aluminum silicate, sodium silicate, sodium aluminum silicate, calcium silicate, calcium aluminum silicate)	talc (a form of magnesium silicate) may be contaminated with asbestos, which is suspected of causing gastrointestinal cancer; some silicates may cause kidney damage, but most are considered biologically inactive	salt, garlic & onion salt, dry mixes, icing sugar (as an anti-caking agent), candy (as a glazing/polishing & release agent), rice (as a coating), chewing gum (as a dusting agent)
propylene glycol (an extraction solvent)	anatomical deformities; reduced growth	salt, flavours, extracts, essences, colours
1, 3-butylene glycol (an extraction solvent)	stimulation of the nervous system; respiratory failure; kidney damage	flavours, flavouring preparations

mineral oil (a release agent)	interference with the body's utilization of the fat-soluble vitamins A, D, E & K	candy, bakery goods, fresh fruits & vegetables
paraffin wax (a coating)	effects on gastrointestinal tract, including links with stomach cancer	fresh fruits & vegetables, cheese
shellac (a glaze)	effects on gastrointestinal tract	cake decorations, candy
polyvinylpyrrolidone (a clarifying agent)	tumour production; liver and kidney damage; spontaneous abortions	ale, beer, cider, wine
methylene chloride (an extraction solvent)	chemically related to known carcinogens	coffee (from the decaffeination process), spice extracts, hop extracts
xylitol (a sweetener)	suspected carcinogen	chewing gum

This list represents about 20 percent of the 350-odd food additives permitted in Canada (not including the hundreds of flavours). It should be noted that roughly the same number of additives has been removed from use in Canadian food since 1964, when our food laws assumed their present form. Over the same period, a similar number of new additives has found its way into the food supply.

Listing these suspicious additives opens up a whole Pandora's box of related questions:

● Can the whole "witches' brew" of additives have a greater effect than the sum of the effects of individual additives? Put another way, what about the *synergy* (chemical interaction producing heightened effects) of food additives with each other and with food ingredients? For example, the preservatives BHA and BHT stimulate the liver to produce certain enzymes that may hasten the destruction and reduce the effectiveness of certain drugs. Furthermore, can food additives react with air and water pollutants invading our bodies to produce heightened toxic effects? Or can additive effects be aggravated by ill health? In this light, no additive has been *really* tested.

"...it is becoming increasingly apparent that a level of exposure to a substance may be free of risk under one set of circumstances but not under another. Permissible levels of exposure have been derived for toxic substances on an isolated basis. The impact of collective exposure to the broad spectrum of toxic substances at or below the permissible levels at which each is viewed as safe demands serious consideration. This will be a most difficult chore since, as yet, we have had little success in defining the effects of 'so-called' isolated exposure to low levels of individual contaminants."

DAVID V. BATES, *Policies and Poisons*
Science Council of Canada, Report No. 28,
October 1977.

● Can smoking aggravate the effects of some food additives in the way that it aggravates harm done by, for instance, oral contraceptives and asbestos dust? (Little is known on this issue.)

● What proportion of mental disorders (behavioural effects) can be attributed to food additives? (Laboratory tests on animals check primarily for physical effects.)

● Would we be safe if all additives were indigestible—that is, if they passed through the digestive system and were never absorbed into the body? (This effect is being explored in the United States with respect to some colourings and preservatives. The problem is to retain the desired effect of the additive while rendering it, now digestible, into indigestible form.)

Action on Suspicious Food Additives

Ideally, the additives of questionable safety listed above should be removed from food in Canada. While we cannot be one hundred percent sure that they are all harmful to human health, is it not preferable to err on the side of caution? Today's rigorous laboratory tests should be applied to *all* additives that have not yet undergone these tests. Any longstanding additives that show harmful effects should then be removed from the food supply.

" ... Though human-made chemicals in food probably constitute only a small part of the diet-cancer complex, their exact contribution to cancer rates is a conspicuous unknown, and some unpleasant surprises are likely in store. The only certainty is that citizens in the wealthiest countries ingest a few thousand different chemical compounds, most of which have not yet been adequately tested for links to cancer, genetic mutations, birth defects or behavioral problems.

"Suspect food additives and pesticide residues are being scrutinized in laboratories, and a few chemicals once assumed safe have been banned in one country or another. But the number of both old and new substances that need to be examined overtaxes the global testing capacity. Newly introduced additives are subjected to fairly rigorous testing, but once the food industry starts producing and people start buying a product, its removal becomes far more difficult politically. When test results are ambiguous, as they often are, and when the probability of cancerous effects on human beings appears slight, as it often does, the economic and political pressures to give a profitable product the benefit of the doubt can seem irresistible."

ERIK P. ECKHOLM, *The Picture of Health: Environmental Sources of Disease* (New York: W. W. Norton, 1977).

FOUR

Federal Food for Thought

How Ottawa Regulates Food Additives

Food Safety

"No person shall sell an article of food that has in or upon it any poisonous or harmful substance."

Section 4 of the *Food and Drugs Act*

Keep this law in mind as we now proceed to discuss the regulation of food safety in Canada.

The statute governing which chemicals are permitted in Canadian food, under what conditions and at what levels, is the *Food and Drugs Act and Regulations*. This is a weighty document (two inches thick) which you may purchase for a mere $38.00 or browse through in the reference section of some public libraries. The regulations are undergoing constant revision at the Health Protection Branch of Health and Welfare Canada. (This act and others may be obtained by writing: Canadian Government Publishing Centre, Supply and Services Canada, Hull, Quebec, K1A 0S9.)

While not all the roughly 350 permitted food additives (excluding flavours) have been tested for safety by today's rigorous methods, all proposed additions to the food additive tables must now be subjected to such tests. It was not until 1964 that these tests became a legal requirement. These tests:

● are carried out by the food manufacturer wishing to use the new chemical (Is this a trustworthy setup? Some sources think not—see box).

"The overwhelming bulk of benefit and risk data, on the basis of which most regulatory decisions are based, comes from the industries being regulated. These data are either generated and interpreted by in-house scientists or by commercial laboratories and universities under contract. In-house scientific staff are not immune to pressures from research and development and marketing departments anxious to hurry their product or process into commerce. Industrial contracts with commercial laboratories and universities are usually awarded secretly.... The contractee, anxious about the award of future contracts, is also not immune to unspoken pressures to produce information or interpretations consistent with the perceived interests of the contracting industry....

"Constraints on data, from gross inadequacy, biased interpretation, manipulation, suppression and outright destruction, are commonplace, especially when profitable products or processes are involved. Evidence of such constraints now justifies *a priori* reservations about the validity of data developed by institutions or individuals whose economic interests are affected, especially when the data base has been maintained as confidential at industry's insistence."

SAMUEL S. EPSTEIN, Professor of Occupational and Environmental Medicine, School of Public Health, University of Illinois, Chicago, in *The Politics of Cancer* (San Francisco: Sierra Club Books, 1978).

● must be carried out on at least two species of animals and must include biochemical and physiological tests, subacute and chronic toxicity studies, and reproductive studies.

● if judged to be reasonable grounds for permitting the chemical in food, lead to the establishment of a safe level for that chemical. Since humans are often more sensitive to foreign chemicals than are test animals, a margin of safety of 100 is used; no level higher than 1% (1/100) of that dosage causing no effect in the test animals may be used in food.* Vigorous proponents of food additives sometimes claim that this margin-of-safety approach is ill-founded since high doses of just about anything will cause cancer and/or death. This claim is simply not supportable.

Canadian food regulations state specifically both what foods may contain a certain additive and the levels at which it is permitted. Here's an example (ppm stands for *parts per million* parts of food):

Column I Additive	Column II Permitted in or Upon	Column III Purposes of Use	Column IV Maximum Level of Use
Magnesium Carbonate	(1) Flour, Whole Wheat Flour	(1) Carrier of benzoyl peroxide	(1) 900 ppm
	(2) Flour, Whole Wheat Flour	(2) Carrier of potassium bromate	(2) 150 ppm
	(3) Confectionery	(3) Release agent	(3) *Good Manufacturing Practice*

* Other data which must accompany an application for use of a new food additive include: information in support of the claimed physical or other technical effect; a statement of the amount of additive proposed and a suggested maximum limit for its residues in the "finished" food; an acceptable analytical method suitable for regulatory purposes, if required by the Health Protection Branch.

Ahah! Our first legal loophole—"Good Manufacturing Practice." Where the limit prescribed for the use of a food additive is stated to be Good Manufacturing Practice, "the amount of the food additive added to a food in manufacturing and processing shall not exceed the amount required to accomplish the purpose for which that additive is permitted to be added to that food" (Section B.01.044 of the *Food and Drug Regulations*). In other words, "whatever is needed to do the job." But the situation is not as chaotic as the definition may lead one to expect. The Health Protection Branch has a large squad of inspectors stationed all over the country who do regular, unannounced checks of all food processing plants to see that they are using food additives within the permissible limits, and who patrol border crossings to check food being imported into Canada. On the other hand, while the inspector's away, the processors may play...(see box). There are plans to eliminate the Good Manufacturing Practice provision in the near future, in cases where it is deemed possible to replace G.M.P. with a maximum permitted level for an additive.

Another legal loophole is of the "sin of omission" variety. So you've heard about the controversy over the flavour enhancer monosodium glutamate (MSG)? Try to find MSG in the *Food and Drug Regulations*! Give up; it's not there. Neither are disodium guanylate, disodium inosinate and other flavour enhancers, since the law does not include them under the definition of "food additive." (They *are*, however, listed in an internationally recognized compendium called the *Food Chemicals Codex*.) At present, *there are no restrictions on the quantities of*

"In the nine months from October 1976 to June 1977, the Health Protection Branch ordered 55 food manufacturers to take products off the market. None of the 55 was prosecuted. Branch chief Dr. Alex Morrison says that a primary reason that food manufacturers are rarely prosecuted in the courts is concern for the reputation of the companies. Nevertheless, during the same nine-month period, government food inspectors did take 22 food manufacturers to court, mostly in cases involving food 'unfit for human consumption.' Fines ranged from $100 to $7500. Also in the same period, inspectors blocked 81 shipments of food into Canada, including 31 for illegal food additives."

SYLVIA WRIGHT, *The Whig-Standard*,
Kingston, Ontario, November 29, 1977.

flavour enhancers used in Canadian food, nor on the kinds of foods that may contain these seasonings. Similarly, *permitted levels for flavourings are absent from the Food and Drug Regulations and most flavourings are not even listed at all.* Try to find artificial ("simulated," "imitation") apple, onion, cheese or maple flavouring, for instance.

The World Health Organization (WHO) regularly issues bulletins relating to the safety of selected food additives. It is up to each country to weigh its own data concerning a specific food additive against the WHO data, and decide whether or not to continue to permit its use. Below is shown a list of those additives that have been withdrawn from use in Canadian food since 1964:

Additive	Uses
saccharin, ammonium saccharin, calcium saccharin, sodium saccharin	non-nutritive sweetener
trichloroethylene (ethylene trichloride)	spices and decaffeinated coffees
chloro I.P.C.	anti-sprouting agent
4 chloro-phenoxy acetic acid	anti-sprouting agent
cyclohexylsulphamic acid	non-nutritive sweetener
diethylpyrocarbonate	malt liquors
maleic hydrazide	anti-sprouting agent
methyl ester of α naphthalene acetic acid	anti-sprouting agent
nonyl alcohol	anti-sprouting agent
bead oil	wine
benzoyl violet 4B	food colour
calcium cyclamate (calcium cyclohexyl sulfamate)	non-nutritive sweetener
chlortetracycline	fish
cobaltous acetate	malt liquors
cobaltous chloride	malt liquors
cobaltous sulphate	malt liquors
cholic acid	dried egg whites

desoxycholic acid	dried egg whites
guinea green B	food colour
light green SF yellowish	food colour
magnesium bicarbonate	variety of foods
magnesium cyclamate (magnesium cyclohexyl sulfamate)	non-nutritive sweetener
naphthol yellow	food colour
nitrosyl chloride	flour
nordihydroguaiaretic acid	anti-oxidant (preservative)
ox bile extract	dried egg whites
oxides of nitrogen	flour
oxytetracycline	fish
potassium cyclamate (potassium cyclohexyl sulfamate)	non-nutritive sweetener
potassium iodide	bakery products
sodium cyclamate sodium cyclohexyl sulfamate)	non-nutritive sweetener
sodium taurocholate	dried egg whites
taurocholic acid	dried egg whites

There are as many different official assessments of food additives as there are countries. We have already mentioned red food colours. The Canadian government's positions on amaranth (U.S. red dye no. 2) and on the preservative nitrite in cured meats are found in Appendix A and B respectively. Several additives permitted in Canada are banned in the nine countries of the European Economic community (Belgium, Denmark, Federal Republic of Germany, France, Ireland, Italy, Luxembourg, the

Netherlands and the United Kingdom)—for example, the colours brilliant blue FCF, iron oxide, and titanium dioxide. The German Federal Republic banned all flour bleaching agents back in the 1950s.

United States food laws include a clause introduced in 1958 (the "Delaney clause") which reads: "No additive shall be deemed to be safe if it is found to induce cancer when ingested by man or animal." Canada has no such clause; it is felt that Section 4 of the *Food and Drugs Act* (above) is good enough.

Labelling

"The following information shall be shown grouped together on any part of the label: Where a prepackaged product consists of more than one ingredient, a list of all ingredients, including, subject to section B.01.009, components, if any."

Section B.01.008 (b) of the *Food and Drug Regulations.*

Looks great! But appearances can be deceiving.

The statutes governing ingredient labelling on food packages are the *Food and Drugs Act and Regulations* and the *Consumer Packaging and Labelling Act and Regulations.* The labelling provisions of these Acts are administered by Consumer and Corporate Affairs Canada.

With regard to the listing of food additives on labels, you should be aware of:

- what must be listed on the label
- what is not required on the label
- what items do not even require a label at all

Ingredients must be listed on the label in descending order of weight. Those ingredients which may be shown at the end of the list *in any order* are: spices, seasonings, herbs (except salt); natural and artificial flavours; flavour enhancers; food additives; vitamins and their salts or derivatives; minerals and their salts. You therefore never really know how much azodicarbonamide is in that loaf of bread....

Before March 1976 many foods (the so-called "standardized foods") were not required to list ingredients on their labels *at all*. Ice cream was just that, for all we were to know, unless we delved into the *Food and Drug Regulations* to discover the flavourings, colourings, pH adjusting agents, stabilizing agents, and sequestering agents that are all part of what the law calls ice cream. So we are much better informed now than we could have been five years ago.

All (well, almost all) ingredients in the food must be listed on the label, yet actual ingredients used (such as the type of shortening or sweetener) may vary from week to week or month to month. So you will find that a label may use such wording as "coconut oil and/or beef tallow," or "sugar (may also contain dextrose)".

Then there's the mystery of the "silent label." Section B.01.009 of the *Food and Drug Regulations,* referred to above, lists a cornucopia of ingredients the components of which may remain mute. So if your favourite food contains any of the following ingredients, you never really know what they're make up of: food colours, flavours, flavour enhancers, margarine, flour, salt, cocoa, vegetable oil, and so on—most of which, incidentally, are or contain what are legally defined as food additives.

In light of the controversy surrounding the safety of food colours, isn't it ironic that food labels won't tell us what we need to know about colour in food. If you are allergic to sunset yellow FCF, knowing that a food contains "colour" is next to useless. Although a consumer may not meet resistance when he or she asks for specifics from a food manufacturer, *there is no requirement that the manufacturer divulge information beyond what is listed on the label.* (For the historical perspective on this issue, see box.)

Other "ingredients" of food which you won't find on the label:

- the mineral oil that greases the pan in which bread and other bakery products are baked.

- unintentional (incidental) additives: primarily agricultural residues of herbicides, insecticides, fertilizers, hormones, and antibiotics that are the tools of "modern" farming. And don't forget the air and water pollutants (such as polychlorinated biphenyls or PCBs) that also find their way into our food.

- chemicals which migrate from the packaging materials into the food. Some of these are deliberate; for example, preservatives added to breakfast cereal packages migrate into the food itself. But some are incidental.

We'll look at these last two issues in greater detail in Appendix F.

" ... Although most ingredients, when declared on a label, must be listed by their specific names, a number of group names such as *'colour,'* 'vegetable oil,' and 'hydrolyzed vegetable protein' have been accepted. ...

"It has been decided that the labels of food products should carry a declaration of ingredients *as soon as may be feasible. ...*

"This decision is based on the premise that *the consumer has the right to know what ingredients are present in foods* and that there is a particular need for those consumers who suffer from food allergy or intolerance to avoid certain ingredients. It is our view that *ingredients should be declared in a manner which is meaningful to the consumer, and as far as is practicable, specific common names rather than functional or group names should be used."* [The italics used above are mine.]

Trade Information Letter 310, March 27, 1969, from the federal Food and Drug Directorate to all food manufacturers.
Well? Twelve years have passed and we still have "food colour" in our food. What's up?

There are several categories of food items which *are not required to list ingredients at all:*

- items packaged from bulk on the premises of a retail store (for example, cheese cut from a wheel or block).

- bakery products baked on the retail premises.

- meat and poultry products that are barbecued, roasted or broiled on the retail premises.

- alcoholic beverages and vinegar.

- individual portions of food served by a restaurant with meals or snacks (for example, mustard, ketchup).

- individual servings of food sold in automatic vending machines or mobile canteens.

- "one-bite" candies.

The rationale for not requiring a list of ingredients for, say, a loaf of bread baked at the supermarket is that a store employee should be able to provide such a list of ingredients. Try asking for it sometime. (Shouldn't the onus be on the store to display this information rather than on the consumer to ask for it?)

Of course, requiring labels that "talk" won't necessarily mean fewer additives in our food, although manufacturers, disturbed by the length of a thorough list of ingredients, might be embarrassed into cutting out the less-than-necessary additives.

"Pure," "Wholesome," "Natural" — Glory Be!

Why does Sealtest market "The All Natural Ice Cream"? Because they think that consumers think if it's natural, it's good for you. Frankly, nothing could be further from the truth. Would you trust an all-natural extract of wild mushrooms? If not, then there is no reason to trust carrageenan in "all natural" ice cream simply because the additive is extracted from seaweed instead of being concocted in a laboratory. The source of a food additive is not nearly as important as whether or not it is actually necessary in the product and whether or not it has harmful effects. (Sealtest's "All Natural" Vanilla ice cream contains: milk solids, liquid sugar (cane), corn syrup, *flavour, carob bean gum, guar gum, karaya gum, carrageenan, mono- and diglycerides, annatto colour.* Compare with Beatrice "Olde Fashioned Recipe" vanilla ice cream: milk solids, cream, sugar, egg yolk, vanilla extract.)

Other words of glorification such as "pure" and "wholesome" are equally deceptive. By law, *all* food must be "pure" in the sense of being unadulterated, according to Section 4(d) of the *Food and Drugs Act.* (A dictionary definition of "adulterated" is "falsified by admixture of baser ingredients.") Consumer and Corporate Affairs Canada does not encourage food manufacturers to use these words on food packages. The government's involvement in the "natural question" is discussed in Appendix E.

On a related topic, a word of warning is in order regarding processed "health" ("natural") foods. In the past ten years, there has been a surge of new food products that cater to the health-conscious consumer. Read their labels—many have additives. For example, some brands of "granola bars" have preservatives and some have artificial colour or flavour.

On the Menu
The Canadian Restaurant and Foodservices Association estimates that we now spend 30 to 35 percent of our food dollars on food consumed outside the home, as opposed to only 17 percent a decade

ago. The percentage of our food bill spent in restaurants, cafeterias and fast food outlets will probably exceed 50 percent by 1984.

The use of additives in restaurant foods (the ingredients of which are not easily accessible to the diner) opens another can of worms (so to speak!). For example, the flavour enhancer MSG is widely used in restaurants to "hold flavour" over long periods of time. As much as one-quarter of the population may suffer adverse reactions to MSG. Also, many restaurants buy ready-made meals (that is, foods not prepared on the premises); some of these have additives.

"McDonald's Restaurants of Canada Ltd. dumped its entire stock of packaged cherry pies earlier this year when government food inspectors found they contained a synthetic red dye (No. 40) prohibited in Canada.

"McDonald's Restaurants has no explanation for the presence of the prohibited ... dye. ...

"Gary Reinblatt of the company's marketing department told the *Whig-Standard:* 'I honestly don't know how it got there. I think you should talk to the president.'

"George Cohon, the president, would not confirm that the pies contained the dye—although that fact is published as public information in the quarterly report of food enforcement activities by Health and Welfare Canada. ..."

SYLVIA WRIGHT, *The Whig-Standard,*
Kingston, Ontario, November 29, 1977.

FIVE

Sounding the Additive Alert

Food is our lifeblood, the ultimate source of all human energy. If we really want healthier food, free from additives of questionable merit, we must be prepared to voice our concerns. What follows is a directory of ways to do that.

The Legislative Approach

Let government know what bothers you about our current food laws. You have a right to know what is in your food and whether it is safe there!

With concerns about food additive safety, write:

Dr. A. B. Morrison
Assistant Deputy Minister*
Health Protection Branch
Health and Welfare Canada
Ottawa, Ontario   K1A 0L2

---

*The current Minister of Health and Welfare is Monique Bégin.

56

"How long I been on chemicals, man? My mother started me off on canned baby food, that's how long."

With concerns about labelling of additives on food packages, write:

Kathleen Francoeur Hendriks
Assistant Deputy Minister*
Consumer Affairs
Consumer and Corporate Affairs Canada
Ottawa, Ontario   K1A 0C9

*The current Minister of Consumer and Corporate Affairs is André Ouellet.

Play the carbon copy game. Send copies of your letters to the Minister responsible, your Member of Parliament (no stamp necessary), your local newspaper, and the offending company (if applicable).

These government departments have regional offices which you can contact by telephone. Look for them in your phone directory.

Want to have a question about food additives raised in the House of Commons? Write to the health critics of the federal opposition parties. They are (at present):

William Blaikie
NDP—MP,
Winnipeg—Bird's Hill
House of Commons
Ottawa, Ontario
K1A 0C6

James McGrath
PC—MP,
St. John's East
House of Commons
Ottawa, Ontario
K1A 0C6

The Supermarket Approach

Let your supermarket know that you want it to stock more additive-free foods. Talk to the store manager and write to the president at the store chain's head office:

Canada Safeway Ltd.
Mr. A. G. Anselmo,
President
535—10th Avenue West
Calgary, Alberta
T2P 2J4

Dominion Stores Ltd.
Mr. T. G. Bolton,
President
605 Rogers Road
Toronto, Ontario
M6M 1B9

Food City (The Oshawa
Group Limited)
Mr. R. D. Wolfe,
President
125 The Queensway
Toronto, Ontario
M8Y 1H7

The Great Atlantic &
Pacific Company of
Canada Ltd. (A & P)
Mr. F. C. Kennedy,
President
P.O. Box 68, Station A
Toronto, Ontario
M5W 1A6

IGA (The Oshawa
Group Limited)
Mr. R. D. Wolfe,
President
125 The Queensway
Toronto, Ontario
M8Y 1H7

Loblaws Limited
Mr. D. A. Nichol,
President
22 St. Clair Avenue East
Toronto, Ontario
M4T 2S5

Miracle Food Mart
(Steinberg's Limited)
Mr. M. A. Dobrin,
President
1500 Atwater Avenue
Montreal, Quebec
H3Z 1Y3

The O.K. Economy
Stores
(Division of Westfair
Foods Limited)
Mr. A. P. Smith,
General Manager
2935 Melville Street
Saskatoon,
Saskatchewan
S7J 0R1

Overwaitea Limited
Mr. Clarence Heppell,
President
7979 Enterprise Street
North Burnaby, B.C.
V5A 1V7

Sobeys Stores Limited
Mr. D. F. Sobey,
President
115 King Street
Stellarton, Nova Scotia
B0K 1S0

Steinberg's Limited
Mr. M. A. Dobrin
President
1500 Atwater Avenue
Montreal, Quebec
H3Z 1Y3

Zehr's (Zehrmart
Ltd.)
Mr. C. M. Zinkan
120 Ottawa Street North
Kitchener, Ontario
N2G 4E7

Super Valu (Kelly,
Douglas & Co. Ltd.)
Mr. R. J. Addington,
President
4700 Kingsway
South Burnaby, B.C.
V6B 3S1

The Food Company Approach

Write to the company with your comments about
what is in—and isn't in—their food. Compliments
are as important as gripes. Some of the large processors are:

Associated Biscuits of
Canada Ltd.
122 O'Connor Drive
Toronto, Ontario
M4B 2T7

Beatrice Foods Ltd.
P.O. Box 1508
Kingston, Ontario
K7L 5C7

Borden Company Ltd.
1275 Lawrence Ave. E.
Don Mills, Ontario
M3A 1C5

Brooke Bond Foods
Limited
16700 Trans-Canada
Highway
Kirkland, Quebec
H9H 3K9

Burns Foods Limited
4195 Dundas Street W.
Toronto, Ontario
M8X 1Y4

Canadian Canners Ltd.
44 Hughson Street S.
Hamilton, Ontario
L8N 3K6

Cadbury Schweppes
Powell Ltd.
100 Alexis Nihon Blvd.,
6th Floor
St. Laurent, Quebec
H4M 2N6

Carnation Co. Ltd.
4174 Dundas Street W.
Toronto, Ontario
M8X 1X4

Canada Bread Division
of Corporate Foods Ltd.
1243 Islington Avenue
Toronto, Ontario
M8X 2W1

Catelli Limited
1200 Plaza Alexis Nihon
1500 Atwater,
Montreal, Quebec
H3Z 1V5

Canada Packers Limited
95 St. Clair Avenue W.
Toronto, Ontario
M4V 1P2

Christie Brown &
Company Ltd.
2150 Lake Shore Blvd. W.
Toronto, Ontario
M8V 1A3

Canada Starch
Company Limited
Best Foods Division
1 Place du Commerce
Nun's Island
Montreal, Quebec
H3E 1A7

Club House Foods
Ltd.
P.O. Box 788
London, Ontario
N6A 4Z2

Dainty Foods Limited
541 Kipling
Toronto, Ontario
M8Z 5E7

Dominion Dairies
Ltd.
(Sealtest Foods)
235 Walmer Road
Toronto, Ontario
M5R 2Y1

General Bakeries
Ltd.
75 The Donway West
Don Mills, Ontario
M3C 2E9

General Foods Limited
2200 Yonge Street
Toronto, Ontario
M5W 1J6

General Mills Canada
Limited
P.O. Box 505
1330 Martin Grove Rd.
Rexdale, Ontario
M9W 4X4

Gerber Products of
Canada Limited
4174 Dundas Street W.
Toronto, Ontario
M8X 1X4

Green Giant of Canada
Limited
500 Ouellette Avenue
Metro Trust Building
Windsor, Ontario
N9A 1B6

H.J. Heinz Company of
Canada Ltd.
250 Bloor Street East
Toronto, Ontario
M4W 1G1

Hygrade Foods Inc.
330 Guizot Street West
Montreal, Quebec
H2P 1L6

Interbake Foods Ltd.
33 Connell Court
Toronto, Ontario
M8Z 1E9

Kellogg Salada Canada
Limited
6700 Finch Avenue W.
Rexdale, Ontario
M9W 5P2

Maple Leaf Mills Ltd.
2300 Yonge Street
Toronto, Ontario
M4P 1E4

Kitchens of Sara Lee
(Canada) Ltd.
379 Orenda Road
Bramalea, Ontario
L6T 1G6

McCain Foods Limited
Florenceville N.B.
E0J 1K0

Kraft Foods Limited
P.O. Box 6118
Montreal, Quebec
H3C 3J3

McNair Products
Company Limited
175 The West Mall
Etobicoke, Ontario
M9C 1C2

Lawry's Foods of
Canada Limited
95 Advance
Toronto, Ontario
M8Z 2T2

Monarch Fine Foods
Company Ltd.
195 Belfield Road
Rexdale, Ontario
M9W 1G9

Thomas J. Lipton Ltd.
2180 Yonge Street
Toronto, Ontario
M4S 2C4

Morrison Lamothe
Frozen Foods
399 Evans
Toronto, Ontario
M8Z 1K9

Mother Parker's Foods
Limited
2350 Stanfield Road
Mississauga, Ontario
L4Y 1S4

Ovaltine Food Products
1377 Lawrence Ave. E.
Don Mills, Ontario
M3A 3M4

Nabob Foods Limited
Lake City
Burnaby B.C.
V5A 3A3

Pillsbury Canada Ltd.
2300 Yonge St., Ste 805
Toronto, Ontario
M4P 1E4

National Sea Products
Limited (High Liner
Division)
85 The East Mall
Toronto, Ontario
M8Z 5W4

Procter & Gamble Co.
of Canada Ltd.
Box 355, Station A
2 St. Clair Avenue West
Toronto, Ontario
M5W 1C5

Nestlé (Canada) Limited
1185 Eglinton Avenue
East
Don Mills, Ontario
M3C 3C7

Quaker Oats Co. of
Canada Ltd.
Quaker Park
Peterborough, Ontario
K9J 7B2

Newfoundland
Margarine Co. Ltd.
250 LeMarchant Road
St. John's,
Newfoundland
A1C 5M5

RJR Foods Limited
365 Evans
Toronto, Ontario
M8Z 5W7

Robin Hood Multifoods
Limited
6600 Côte des Neiges
P.O. Box 8505
Montreal, Quebec
H3C 3P1

Standard Brands Ltd.
550 Sherbrooke Street W.
Montreal, Quebec
H3A 1B9

W.H. Schwartz & Sons
Limited
P.O. Box 790
Halifax, Nova Scotia
B3J 2R9

Unico Foods Limited
8000 Keele Street
Concord, Ontario
L4K 1B1

Shopsy's Foods Limited
2 Huxley Road
Weston, Ontario
M9M 1H1

Weetabix of Canada
Ltd.
6101 Yonge Street
Willowdale, Ontario
M2M 3W4

Many of these companies belong to an association of food manufacturers. Got a general beef, an overall point of view?
Write:

Philip Moyes, Acting President
Grocery Products Manufacturers of Canada
1185 Eglinton Ave. E., Suite 101
Don Mills, Ontario
M3C 3C6

The Eating Out Approach

The quality of restaurant food and institutional food is largely a municipal responsibility, usually co-ordinated at the provincial level. With complaints and comments, write:

Alberta:	Department of Social Services and Community Health Administration Building Edmonton, Alberta T5K 2B6
British Columbia:	Ministry of Health Parliament Buildings Victoria, British Columbia V8V 1X4
Manitoba:	Ministry of Health and Social Development Room 200, 185 Carlton Street Winnipeg, Manitoba R3C 3J1
Newfoundland:	Department of Health Confederation Building St. John's, Newfoundland A1C 5T7
New Brunswick:	Department of Health Centennial Building Fredericton, New Brunswick E3B 5H1
Nova Scotia:	Department of Health Joseph Horne Building Granville at Prince P.O. Box 488 Halifax, Nova Scotia B3J 2R8

Ontario:	Ministry of Health Queen's Park Toronto, Ontario M7A 1E9
Prince Edward Island:	Department of Health Box 3000 Charlottetown, P.E.I. C1A 4A0
Quebec:	Ministère des Affaires Sociales 1975 Chemin Ste.-Foy Québec, Québec G1S 2M1
Saskatchewan:	Department of Public Health Provincial Health Building Regina, Saskatchewan S4S 0B3

You may wish to deal with the restaurant or institution directly (the best initial approach). Ask what's in their "secret recipes"! And voice your concerns by writing:

René M. Vandervelde, President
Canadian Restaurant and Foodservices Association
80 Bloor Street West
Toronto, Ontario
M5S 2V1

SIX

Not by Additives Alone

A Temporary Antidote

Thinking pragmatically, we must understand that changes to what is in our food won't happen overnight. Laboratory studies to provide proof of health effects from a food additive may take three years or more to complete. The complex bureaucracy that is the federal government often cannot, or will not, move as quickly as we would like it to. Scientific opinions will diverge, industrialists will lobby, consumers will want their say.

So in the meantime, we must work with what we have. You, too, can become a successful supermarket sleuth! Carry this handbook when you shop. Use the index to avoid the worst additives and to be aware of what the others are. Compare different brands of the same food item to show yourself that many additives appear unnecessary. Here are some examples (additives of questionable safety are printed in **bold type**):

"...and...er...*For*-give us this day our daily bread."

Kraft Cracker Barrel Old
Cheddar Cheese
(rennet and/or pepsin
and/or microbial enzyme,
potassium sorbate,
colour, may contain
calcium chloride)

Richmello Extra Old
Cheddar Cheese
(rennet and/or pepsin only)

Crisco Vegetable Oil (dimethylpolysiloxane, **BHA, BHT)**	Unico Vegetable Oil (no additives)
Dominion 100% Whole Wheat Bread (calcium sulphate, ammonium sulphate, mono- and diglycerides, potassium bromate, calcium phosphate tribasic, 1-cysteine hydrochloride, calcium propionate)	Dempster's Whole Earth Bread (no additives)
Kellogg's Corn Flakes **(BHT)**	Post Bran Flakes (no additives)
Sealtest Light 'n' Lively Blueberry Yogurt (gelatin, citric acid, potassium sorbate, **colour, artificial flavour)**	Gay Lea Blueberry Yogurt (no additives)
Dad's Shortcake Cookies (sodium bicarbonate, ammonium bicarbonate, **artificial colour and flavours)**	Peek Freans Shortcake Biscuits (no additives)
Aylmer Tomatoes (calcium sulphate or calcium chloride)	York Tomatoes (no additives)
West Salad Dressing **(calcium disodium EDTA)**	Dominion Salad Dressing (no additives)

Gay Lea Sour Cream
(modified starch,
locust bean gum,
carrageenan, rennet)

Bird's Hill Sour Cream
(no additives)

Heinz Sweet Mixed Pickles
(colour)

Heinz Bread 'n' Butter
Pickles
(no additives)

Jacob's Cream Crackers
(BHA)

McVitie's Tuc Crackers
(no additives)

Kellogg's Rice Krispies
(BHA)

Quaker Puffed Rice
(no additives)

York Smoothy
Peanut Butter
(mono- and diglycerides)

Loblaws Jack & Jill
Peanut Butter
(no additives)

McLaren's Stuffed
Manzanilla Olives
(lactic acid and/or
calcium chloride,
guar gum,
sodium alginate,
potassium sorbate)

Gattuso Olive
Combination
(lactic acid only)

Monarch All
Purpose Flour
(chlorine,
benzoyl peroxide)

Monarch Unbleached
All Purpose
Enriched Flour
(no additives)

Beckers Buttermilk
(buttermilk flavour)

Donlands Buttermilk
(no additives)

FBI Apple Drink
**(artificial and natural
flavour, colour)**

Allen's Apple Juice
(no additives)

Planters Dry Roasted
Peanuts
(**modified starch,
monosodium glutamate,**
gum acacia, **flavour,**
tricalcium phosphate)

Steinberg Salted
Blanched Peanuts
(no additives)

You may be surprised to find that some foods are
freer of additives than might be expected. Tomato
ketchup seldom contains any added colours, flavours, or preservatives. Neither do most jams and
jellies. (However, ketchup may contain as much as
30% sugar, and jams or jellies as much as 60%,
which many would consider a drawback.) Provisions
for additives to those foods are available to food
processors under the *Food and Drug Regulations,*
but often there are no takers.

Watch for indications of the trend toward food
less laced with additives of questionable utility.
Market surveys conducted by Beatrice Foods, a
multinational company headquartered in Chicago,
indicate that 30% of consumers are now prepared to
pay a higher price for food without additives. As
the popularity of such foods increases, economies of
large scale production should come into effect so
that prices will decrease. Beatrice now produces one
of the very few ice creams in Canada without additives—at a price 25% above other ice creams.
Dempster's Bread (a division of Corporate Foods
Limited of Toronto) has marketed its Whole Earth
no-additive bread for several years now—at a price
45% above its other breads.

With increasing consumer concern about additives in foods, we find two opposing responses from

the food processing industry: There is staunch defence of the use of "chemicals", but there is also a move towards foods without them. In between are responses like General Foods' list of products free of tartrazine, a yellow food colour to which some people are allergic; it seems that telling the consumer which products do *not* contain this questionable food dye is considered a customer service. (Presumably, telling us which products *do* contain the colour would be a little too direct.)

Many Canadian towns and cities now offer alternatives to today's supermarket fare for those unwilling to wait for needed changes in mass market food merchandizing. Stores specializing in "natural" foods ("health" foods, "whole" foods) are an increasingly popular alternative. Food in these stores is often more expensive than the equivalent in a supermarket—but if you can purchase food in bulk rather than in prepackaged form, at least excessive packaging is avoided. Personnel in these stores should be able to give you lists of ingredients in bulk foods if you ask for them.

Food co-operatives usually offer the same foods as are found in natural food stores—but with real savings compared to supermarket prices, packaging, and additives (see box). Here the savings accrue through the non-profit orientation and the volunteer labour contributed by members.* As in the case of

* If you're interested in finding out more about food co-ops, read: *The Food Co-Op Handbook* by the Co-Op Handbook Collective (Boston: Houghton Mifflin, 1975) and *The Canadian Whole Food Book* by the Editors of *Harrowsmith* (Camden East, Ont.: Camden House, 1980). Contact: Ontario Federation of Food Co-Ops and Clubs, 58 Wade Ave., Toronto, Ontario, M6H 1P6.

Food	Price		
	Supermarket	Natural Food Store	Food Co-op
whole wheat flour	$0.44/lb.	$0.27/lb.	$0.22/lb.
peanut butter	$1.45/lb.	$1.10/lb.	$1.09/lb.
cheddar cheese (old)	$3.15/lb.	$2.90/lb.	$2.31/lb.
eggs (medium)	$0.98/doz.	$0.95/doz.	$0.89/doz.
rolled oats	$0.45/lb.	$0.32/lb.	$0.29/lb.

Adapted from: Harrowsmith (Editors). *The Canadian Whole Food Book.* Camden East, Ontario: Camden House, 1980, p. 58.

natural food stores, the selection of grocery items is small compared to what fills the centre aisles of supermarkets. But many centre-aisle processed foods are simply convenience items for which substitutes can easily be prepared at home from additive-free ingredients—salad dressings, cakes, cookies, breakfast cereals, spaghetti sauce, puddings, jelly desserts, yoghurt, baby foods, soups, and so on.

While many of us may wish to adopt an additive-free diet to protect ourselves from possible long-term toxicities, it has been claimed that such a diet is essential for the physical and mental health of several groups of people experiencing acute reactions to certain additives. Dr. Ben Feingold, an American allergist and pediatrician, has devised a diet for hyperactive (hyperkinetic) children which, he estimates, will elicit a fully positive response in 50% of cases and benefit to the extent of discontinuing drug therapy in at least 75% of cases. The Feingold diet eliminates all artificial flavours and colours, as well as food high in a group of chemical compounds called salicylates (many fruits, some vegetables, and nuts).

Admittedly, the usefulness of the Feingold diet has come under attack in recent years. Appendix D contains a brief outline of this criticism.

Doctor Michael Lesser, a California psychiatrist, has found that a dramatic improvement in the behaviour of schizophrenics can be achieved simply by avoiding "junk foods," invariably laced with additives. Lesser is one of a growing number of medical people discovering that an improved diet—which usually includes, among other changes, the elimina-

---

"Barbara Reed, the chief probation officer in the city of Cuyahoga Falls, Ohio, reports 'dramatic success' in rehabilitating convicted criminals by changing their diets and increasing their vitamin consumption.

"In the past 2½ years, she says, 250 paroled convicts have been placed on diets that eliminate refined sugar, refined flour, artificial colors and artificial flavors.

"'We have not had a single person back in court for trouble who has stayed on the nutritional diet,' she says."

SYLVIA WRIGHT, *The Whig-Standard,* Kingston, Ontario, November 26, 1977.

tion of most food additives—is an effective medicine for both physical and mental disorders. Such discoveries improve the well-being not only of the individual but often, some in the field claim, of society as well (see box on page 75).

SEVEN

Further Investigation

A Food Additive Information Source List

Government Publications

Consumer and Corporate Affairs Canada. "Let the Labels
Do the Talking." March 1977.

The Consumer Packaging and Labelling Act and Regulations. Supply and Services Canada.

The Food and Drugs Act and Regulations. Supply and
Services Canada. (Under constant revision)

Health and Welfare Canada. *Food Additives (Dispatch
No. 30).* Revised 1977.

Health and Welfare Canada. *Guide to Food Additives.*
1977 (reprinted 1980).

Health and Welfare Canada. "Fact Sheet on Monosodium Glutamate for Consumers." 1979.

Health and Welfare Canada. "Fact Sheet on Monosodium Glutamate for Restaurant and Food Service
Operators." 1979.

Health and Welfare Canada. *Health Protection and Food
Laws.* Revised 1979.

Health and Welfare Canada. *Food Additive Pocket Dictionary.* 1980.

Health and Welfare Canada. *Food Additives—What Do*

You Think?: Highlights of an Opinion Survey, Summer 1979 (Dispatch No. 48). 1980.

Health and Welfare Canada. *Food Additives—What Do You Think?: Report on Opinion Survey Conducted Summer 1979.* 1980.

Health and Welfare Canada. *"Introducing. . . . Food Additives."* 1980.

Health and Welfare Canada. *Food Hang-Ups.* Revised 1981.

KNOX, M. H. and POPE, E. M. (Health Protection Branch, Health and Welfare Canada). "Food Additive Opinion Survey with Canadian Consumers." *Canadian Institute of Food Science and Technology Journal,* vol. 13, no. 2 (April 1980), pp. A10-A13.

MORRISON, A. B. (Health Protection Branch, Health and Welfare Canada). "Proposal on Aspartame." Information Letter No. 564, September 12, 1979.

Food Industry Publications

The availability of industry publications on food additives varies. Please contact individual companies listed in Chapter Five and ask whether they carry any such publications.

Books

BURROS, MARIAN. *Pure and Simple: Delicious Recipes for Additive-Free Cooking.* New York: William Morrow, 1978.

CONNORS, C. KEITH. *Food Additives and Hyperactive Children.* New York: Plenum Press, 1980.

DOYLE, RODGER P. and REDDING, JAMES L. *The Complete Food Handbook.* 3rd. edition. New York: Grove Press, 1979.

ECKHOLM, ERIK P. *The Picture of Health: Environmental Sources of Disease.* New York: W. W. Norton, 1977. (A Project of the Worldwatch Institute, with the support and cooperation of the United Nations Environment Program)

Environmental Defense Fund and Robert H. Boyle. *Malignant Neglect.* New York: Alfred A. Knopf, 1979.

EPSTEIN, SAMUEL S. *The Politics of Cancer.* Revised and Expanded Edition. Garden City, N.Y.: Anchor Press/Doubleday, 1979.

FEINGOLD, BEN. *Why Your Child is Hyperactive.* New York: Random House, 1974.

FEINGOLD, HELENE and FEINGOLD, BEN. *The Feingold Cookbook for Hyperactive Children.* New York: Random House, 1979.

FURIA, THOMAS E. *CRC Handbook of Food Additives.* 2nd. edition. Cleveland: CRC Press, 1972.

GALLI, C. L., PAOLETTI, P. and VETTORAZZI, G. (eds). *Chemical Toxicology of Food.* Amsterdam: Elseveir/North Holland Biomedical Press, 1978.

HALL, ROSS HUME. *Food for Nought: The Decline in Nutrition.* New York: Random House, 1976.

Harrowsmith (eds). *The Canadian Whole Food Book.* Camden East, Ont.: Camden House, 1980.

HUNTER, BEATRICE TRUM. *Additives Book.* New Canaan, Conn.: Keats Publishing, 1980.

____. *Consumer Beware!: Your Food and What's Been Done to It.* New York: Bantam Books, 1971.

____. *The Mirage of Safety: Food Additives and Federal Policy.* New York: Charles Scribner's Sons, 1975.

HUNTER, BEATRICE TRUM (ed). *Food and Your Health.* New Canaan, Conn.: Keats Publishing, 1974.

JACOBSON, MICHAEL F. *Eater's Digest: The Consumer's Factbook of Food Additives.* Garden City, N.Y.: Doubleday, 1976 (updated).

KRUUS, P. and VALERIOTE, I. M. (eds). *Controversial Chemicals: A Citizens Guide.* Montreal: Multiscience Publications Ltd., 1979. (re: caffeine, nitrites and nitrates, and saccharin, plus 22 chemicals that are not direct food additives)

LERZA, CATHERINE and JACOBSON, MICHAEL (eds). *Food for People, Not for Profit: A Source Book on the Food Crisis.* New York: Ballantine Books, 1975.

MACKARNESS, RICHARD. *Chemical Victims.* London: Pan Books, 1980.

National Academy of Sciences—National Research Council. Publication 1406. *Food Chemicals Codex.* 2nd. edition. Washington, D.C.: 1972.

National Farmers Union. *Nature Feeds Us: The Food System from Soil to Table.* Saskatoon: 1976. (Available from: NFU, 250C Second Ave. South, Saskatoon, Saskatchewan, S7K 2M1)

PACKARD, VERNAL S., JR. *Processed Foods and the Consumer.* Minneapolis: University of Minnesota, 1976.

SARJEANT, DORIS D. and EVANS, KAREN S. *The Truth About Food Additives (Including a Complete Alphabetical Guide).* Hampton, N.B., 1980. (To order, send a cheque/money order for $6.95 to Doris Sarjeant and Karen Evans, P.O. Box 58, Hampton, New Brunswick, E0G 1Z0)

TAYLOR, R. J. *Food Additives.* New York: Wiley Interscience, 1980.

WHELAN, ELIZABETH M. and STARE, FREDRICK J. *Panic in the Pantry: Food Facts, Fads and Fallacies.* New York: Atheneum, 1977.

WINTER, RUTH. *A Consumer's Dictionary of Food Additives.* Revised ed. New York: Crown Publishers, 1978.

Articles (and Other Short Publications)

ALLEN, CARROLL. "Additives: Is Ignorance a Bliss We Can Afford?" *Homemaker's*, March, 1980, pp. 6-20.

American Council on Science and Health. *Diet and Hyperactivity: Is There a Relationship?* May 1979. (Pamphlet available for $5.00 from ACSH, 47 Maple Street, Summit, N.J. 07901)

American Council on Science and Health. *Saccharin.* November 1979 and June 1980 (update). (Pamphlets available from ACSH, 47 Maple Street, Summit, N.J. 07901)

American Council on Science and Health. *Cancer in the United States: Is There an Epidemic?* August 1980. (Pamphlet available for $2.00 from ACSH, 47 Maple Street, Summit, N.J. 07901)

ANGELINE, J. F. and LEONARDOS, G. P. "Food Additives: Some Economic Considerations." *Food Technology*, April, 1973, pp. 40-50.

BARNETT, DONNA: "Dr. Alexander Morrison, At Your Civil Service." *Harrowsmith*, no. 16 (1978), pp. 49-61, 74-78, 126.

BRODY, JANE E. "How Wholesome is 'Natural' Food?" *The New York Times*, December 12, 1979.

___. "Natural Isn't Always Better, When It's On a Food Label." *The Globe and Mail (New York Times Service)*, January 23, 1980.

Caccia, Charles. *Food and Additives: What Are We Doing to Our Food?* February 1981. (Booklet available from Charles Caccia, M.P., House of Commons, Ottawa, Ontario, K1A 0A6)

"Canadians Say No to Additives." *Probe Post*, November-December, 1979 (vol. 2 no. 4), p. 3.

Center for Science in the Public Interest. *Chemical Cuisine.* 1977. (A poster about food additive safety, available from CSPI, 1755 S Street N.W., Washington, D.C., 20009; $1.75 each)

Center for Science in the Public Interest. *Does Everything Cause Cancer?: A Food Safety Primer.* 1979. (A booklet available for $1.00 from CSPI, 1755 S Street N.W., Washington, D.C., 20009)

CHRISTOPHER, RITA. "Eating Right." *Maclean's,* November 26, 1979, pp. 49-60.

CIMONS, MARLENE and JACOBSON, MICHAEL. "How to Decode a Food Label." *Mother Jones,* February/March, 1978.

CLARK, WAYNE. "The Great Granola Gold Rush." *The Financial Post Magazine,* October, 1979, pp. 28-36.

COLMAN, ARTHUR D. "Possible Psychiatric Reactions to Monosodium Glutamate." *The New England Journal of Medicine,* vol. 299, no. 16 (October 19, 1978), p. 902.

DICKSON, DAVID. "Chemicals in Food: New US Framework Proposed." *Nature,* vol. 278 (March 8, 1979), p. 110.

ENGEL, JUNE and PARR, ELIZABETH. "Additives: What Are They Doing to Our Food?" *Chatelaine,* March, 1980, pp. 60-64.

Environmental Protection Agency (US Government). *This Rat Died in a Cancer Lab to Save Lives.* January 1980. (Pamphlet). Order from E.P.A., Washington, D.C., 20460.

"The Flowering of the Health Food Industry." *Saturday Night,* May, 1980, pp. 3-6.

"Food Additives." Editorial in *The Lancet,* August 16, 1969, pp. 361-362.

"Food-Additives Market Will Double in 1980s." *Chemical Week,* February 20, 1980, pp. 55-56.

"Food Allergy." Editorial in *The Lancet,* February 3, 1979, pp. 249-250.

FRANCIS, F. J. "Risk/Benefit Problems in Food Safety Assessment". *Journal of the Canadian Dietetic Association,* vol. 40 no. 4 (October, 1979), pp. 274-279.

GARDNER, HUGH. "Sowbelly Blues: The Links Between Bacon and Cancer." *Harrowsmith*, no. 9 (1977), pp. 33-37, 85-92.

HALL, ROSS HUME. "Fabricated Foods: Quality Declines as Technology Takes Over." *Canadian Consumer*, October, 1976, pp. 1-3.

"Health Food Not Always More Nutritious." *Canadian Consumer*, October, 1980, p. 41.

"Irradiated Food: Industry Warms Up to an Old Idea." *Chemical Week*, October 8, 1980, pp. 42-43.

JACOBSON, MICHAEL. "BHT: Weighing the Benefits and Risks." *Nutrition Action*, vol. 4 no. 9 (September 1977), pp. 6-7, 9.

JOHNSON, ANITA. "Unnecessary Chemicals." *Environment*, vol. 20 no. 2 (March 1978), pp. 6-11.

KERMODE, G. O. "Food Additives." *Scientific American*, March, 1972, pp. 15-21.

KOJIMA, KOHEI. "The Toxicological Assessment of Natural Food Colorants." *In:* GALLI, C. L., PAOLETTI P. and VETTORAZZI, G. (eds). *Chemical Toxicology of Food.* Amsterdam: Elsevier/North-Holland Biomedical Press, 1978.

KON, S. H. "Underestimation of Chronic Toxicities of Food Additives and Chemicals: The Bias of a Phantom Rule." *Medical Hypotheses*, vol. 4 (1978), pp. 324-39.

MacNEIL, Shel. "Health-Food Ripoff: Preservatives Found." *The Whig-Standard* (Kingston, Ontario), September 19, 1979.

____. "Health Food Retailers Rely on Suppliers' Word." *The Whig-Standard* (Kingston, Ontario), September 21, 1979.

"Most Cooked Bacon Free of Nitrosamines." *Chemical Week*, July 9, 1980.

"Nitrites and Nitrosamines: Is the Hot Dog an Endangered Species?" *Consumer Reports*, May, 1980, pp. 310-311.

PIM, LINDA R. "I Have Gouda News and I Have Bad News." *Harrowsmith*, no. 12 (1978), pp. 109-110.

ROBERTSON, DAVID; BEALL, MOYA; and SCHMIDT, PAUL. "Richest of the Enriched." *Harrowsmith*, no. 24 (1979), pp. 27-37. (re: additives in bread)

SCHELL, ORVILLE. "What This Country Needs Is a Stronger White Rat: Inside the Food Technology Bazaar." *Mother Jones*, February/March, 1979.

Science Council of Canada. *Policies and Poisons: The Containment of Long-Term Hazards to Human Health in the Environment and in the Workplace.* Ottawa: October 1977. Report No. 28.

STARE, F. J., WHELAN, E. M. and SHERIDAN, MARGARET. "Diet and Hyperactivity: Is There a Relationship?" *Pediatrics*, vol. 66, no. 4 (October 1980), pp. 521-525.

TEPPER, L. B. "Chemicals, the Consumer and Credibility." *Food and Cosmetics Toxicology*, vol. 12 (1974), pp. 237-241.

THOMASSON, W. A. "Dangerous to Your Health: Saccharin, Cancer and the Delaney Clause." *Atlantic Monthly*, June, 1979, pp. 25-26.

"What Do Consumers Want to See on Food Labels?" *Consumer Reports*, October, 1979, p. 591.

WHELAN, ELIZABETH M. and SMITH, TERRENCE. "Of Mice and Men—and Risk in Foods." *Across the Board*, March, 1980, pp. 74-81.

WRIGHT, SYLVIA. *Food and Your Health*. Kingston, Ont.: The Whig-Standard, 1978. (A series of articles in booklet form, available from: The Whig-Standard, 302-310 King Street, Kingston, Ontario, K7L 4Z7; $2.00 each)

WOLFF, I. A. and WASSERMAN. A. E. "Nitrates, Nitrites and Nitrosamines." *Science*, July 7, 1972, pp. 15-18.

ZANUSSI, CARLO. "Allergenic Potential of Food Additives." *In:* GALLI, C.L., PAOLETTI, P. and VETTORAZZI, G. (eds.) *Chemical Toxicology of Food.* Amsterdam: Elsevier/North-Holland Biomedical Press, 1978.

ZIEGEL, JACOB S. "The *Food and Drugs Act* and Other Horrors." *Canadian Consumer*, October, 1980, pp. 15-16.

Periodicals

Canadian Consumer (Consumers' Association of Canada). 200 First Avenue, Ottawa, Ontario, K1S 2G6.

Canadian Institute of Food Science and Technology Journal. 46 Elgin Street, Suite 38, Ottawa, Ontario, K1P 5K6.

Consumer Reports (Consumers Union). 256 Washington Street, Mount Vernon, New York, 10550.

En-Trophy Review. The En-Trophy Institute, 20 Hilton Street, Hamilton, Ontario, L8P 3K2.

Food and Agriculture Organization/World Health Organization, Joint Expert Committee on Food Additives. *Evaluation of Certain Food Additives*. Annual Reports. The United Nations.

Food and Cosmetics Toxicology. Pergamon Press, Headington Hill Hall, Oxford, 0X3 0BW, England.

Food Drug Cosmetic Law Journal. 4025 W. Peterson Avenue, Chicago, Illinois, 60646.

Harrowsmith. Camden East, Ontario, K0K 1J0.

Probe Post (Pollution Probe). 12 Madison Avenue, Toronto, Ontario, M5R 2S1.

Organizations

Allergy Information Association, 25 Poynter Drive, Room 7, Weston, Ontario, M9R 1L1.

American Council on Science and Health, 47 Maple Street, Summit, N.J., 07901.

Canadian Food Processors Association, 130 Albert Street, Suite 1409, Ottawa, Ontario K1P 5G4.

Canadian Institute of Food Science and Technology, 46 Elgin Street, Suite 38, Ottawa, Ontario, K1P 5K6.

Canadian Public Health Association, 1335 Carling Avenue, Suite 210, Ottawa, Ontario, K1Z 8N8. (Canadian distributor for publications of the World Health Organization)

Carcinogen Information Program, Webster College, 470 E. Lockwood Ave., St. Louis, Missouri, 63119.

Center for Science in the Public Interest, 1755 S Street N.W., Washington, D.C., 20009.

Consumers Union, 256 Washington Street, Mount Vernon, New York, 10550.

Consumers' Association of Canada, 200 First Avenue, Ottawa, Ontario, K1S 2G6. (Has provincial and local units as well)

Grocery Products Manufacturers of Canada, 1185 Eglinton Avenue East, Suite 101, Don Mills, Ontario M3C 3C6.

Human Ecology Foundation of Canada, R.R. #1, Goodwood, Ontario, L0C 1A0.

Pollution Probe, 12 Madison Avenue, Toronto, Ontario, M5R 2S1.

Films, Slide Shows, Radio

Alice in Additiveland. A slide/tape and filmstrip/tape production by the Health Protection Branch of Health and Welfare Canada. Contact their local offices for distribution details.

A Chemical Feast. Educational Broadcasting Corporation, 1973. Produced by National Educational Television. Released in Canada by Marlin Motion Pictures; 11 minutes, sound and colour.

Canadian Broadcasting Corporation (CBC). *The Food Show.* 8:30 to 9:00 A.M., Sunday, local time; produced in Toronto.

Canadian Broadcasting Corporation (CBC). *Radio Noon.*

12 noon to 2:00 P.M., Monday to Friday, local time; locally produced.

Eat, Drink and be Wary. Churchill Productions, 1975. Released in Canada by Gordon Watt Films; 21 minutes, sound and colour.

Government Agencies

Health Protection Branch, Health and Welfare Canada, Ottawa, Ontario K1A 0L2.

Consumer Standards Directorate, Consumer and Corporate Affairs Canada, Ottawa, Ontario, K1A 0C9.

Food and Drug Administration (US Government), 5600 Fishers Lane, Rockville, Maryland, 20857.

APPENDIX A

Canadian Government Position on the Food Colour Amaranth

The following is an excerpt from a press release of February 2, 1976, issued by Health and Welfare Canada.

Ottawa—National Health and Welfare Minister Marc Lalonde today announced that after a careful evaluation of all available evidence, and discussions with health experts in other countries, the Health Protection Branch (HPB) has concluded there is insufficient evidence available at this time to justify the removal of the food colour Amaranth from foods sold in Canada.

The recent decision by the Food and Drug Administration (FDA) of the United States to propose a ban on the use of Amaranth in that country raised legitimate concern among Canadian consumers over its use in this country. This concern, however, is not substantiated by the available scientific evidence.

It should be noted that Amaranth has received repeated approval for use by the Joint Expert Committee of the Food and Agriculture Organization

(FAO) and of the World Health Organization (WHO). Canada was in agreement with the Committee's assessment and the FDA study has not altered our view.

The U.S. decision to ban Amaranth resulted primarily from a study conducted in the FDA's own laboratories.... Rats of both sexes were fed Amaranth ... and a variety of benign and malignant tumors was observed.... From the data available, HPB scientists consider this increase in tumors of no biological significance for the following reasons:

(1) The effect was not organ specific. Experts in the cancer field consider that for a study to have biological significance, it is necessary to demonstrate the presence of a number of tumors of an unusual tumor type for the particular species and strain of animal or an increase in the number of tumors for a particular organ. In both instances the increase would have to be significantly greater than in control animals. The tumors found in the FDA study were similar in number and type to those previously encountered in rats of the same strain and age, reared and housed under similar environmental conditions and fed diets free of the colour.

(2) Amaranth has a chemical structure similar to other dyes that are non-carcinogenic and different from those that are carcinogenic.

(3) The tumor increase was confined to female rats and except for the mammary tumors the cancers were not sex related. This is very unusual, particularly since the number of malignant tumors in control male rats was greater than in male rats given 3

percent Amaranth in the diet. This latter observation could, by the same reasoning apparently used by the FDA, be used as evidence that in male rats, Amaranth actually prevents the production of cancer.

(4) Preliminary mutagenicity screening tests conducted by HPB indicate that Amaranth is not mutagenic [causing genetic changes] and hence not likely to be carcinogenic [causing cancer]. Almost all substances which are known to be mutagenic are also carcinogenic.

(5) In the FDA study, there was a mix-up in the animal numbers and in the diets fed to certain groups of animals. Many tissues were in a state of advanced decomposition making microscopic examination extremely difficult to carry out properly. This would appear to indicate inadequate experimental control, and makes it well-nigh impossible to adequately assess the U.S. study.

Other research in the U.S., not evidently considered by the FDA in its decision-making process, included teratogenic [causing birth defects] studies conducted by Dr. J. Verrett, an FDA staff member. Dr. Verrett expressed particular concern about possible adverse reproductive effects from Amaranth on the C.B.C. program Market Place, January 25, 1976. She stated that Amaranth caused deaths and birth defects in chick embryos. Dr. Verrett's observations are not considered relevant in terms of the safety of Amaranth to humans. The chick embryo is not considered to be a suitable test species by teratologists generally.... The chick embryo technique was replaced in 1966 at HPB by more reliable techniques that employ mammalian species. HPB deplores the fact that C.B.C.—Market Place did not check on the reliability of the chick embryo test. . . .

It is important to point out that HPB has discussed the validity of the FDA rat study with a number of university-based toxicologists and cancer experts in the United States. All those contacted agree with the Canadian assessment of the FDA experiment.

Amaranth is permitted as a food colour in the nine countries of the European Economic Community (EEC), and in Sweden, Japan and many other countries. Its use is not permitted in Russia.

In 1964 the FAO/WHO Joint Expert Committee on Food Additives evaluated the safety of Amaranth on the basis of all the relevant data available at that time. This Committee of international experts concluded that adequate data were available to rule out carcinogenicity of this colour in rats and mice. The Committee established a level of Amaranth (termed the Acceptable Daily Intake or A.D.I.) which if consumed every day throughout the entire life-span would be safe.

In 1972 this Committee reevaluated the safety of Amaranth in the light of new data that had become available. The new data included reports from Russia suggesting carcinogenic effects and fetotoxic [harmful to the fetus] effects in rats. Difficulty in interpreting the results of the Russian studies and the fact that further relevant studies were then in progress caused the Committee to defer a final reevaluation. However, in the interest of prudence, the previous A.D.I. was lowered by 50% and given a temporary status pending results of the work in progress.

After the Russian reports were published, extensive studies were undertaken by HPB scientists and in at least three laboratories in the U.S.A. HPB studies initiated in 1973 and completed in 1974 on the teratogenic and reproductive effects of Amaranth in cats and rats showed the colour to be without adverse effects. Furthermore, none of the U.S. studies produced conclusive evidence that Amaranth caused adverse effects on fetal development. In November 1975 the National Toxicology Advisory Committee in the U.S. reached the conclusion that Amaranth is not fetotoxic.

The FAO/WHO Expert Committee on Food Additives considered Amaranth for a third time in 1975. The Committee confirmed the A.D.I. of Amaranth arrived at in 1972.

As new technology is developed, the safety of Amaranth and other food colours is continually reevaluated by HPB scientists. In studies conducted in our laboratories in the late 1950's, the cancer producing potential of a number of food colours was assessed. Most, including Amaranth, were found to be safe. One of the colours, Ponceau 3R, was found to be carcinogenic and was removed from the Canadian market. This pioneering Canadian research led to the banning of Ponceau 3R throughout the world.

New techniques for assessing the mutagenic effects of chemicals have been developed in recent years and these techniques now are being applied by HPB to the study of Amaranth. To date, all results from these mutagen testing procedures have been negative, giving the strong indication that Amaranth does not induce mutations. . . .

In addition to data developed in our own research laboratories, HPB scientists also have access to published and unpublished reports on Amaranth and an HPB scientist serves on the FAO/WHO Expert Committee mentioned previously. Each time a concern has been raised over some aspect of potential hazard of Amaranth as a food colour, the evidence has been evaluated and, if necessary, additional evidence has been collected.

APPENDIX B

Canadian Government Position on Nitrite in Cured Meats

The following is the full text of a press release issued by Health and Welfare Canada on August 16, 1978.

Ottawa—Health and Welfare Minister Monique Bégin today announced that additional restrictions on the use of nitrite in the curing of meats in Canada are not warranted at this time. The decision was reached following thorough evaluation of available information on the benefits and risks associated with nitrite.

Miss Bégin noted that it has been a long-term policy of her department to limit the use of nitrite and nitrate, a related chemical, to levels necessary to prevent formation of botulinus toxin in cured meat products. The department's long-term goal is to phase out the use of nitrite and nitrate if safe and effective substitutes become available. Thus, use of nitrite in curing fish products was prohibited in 1959. In 1975, almost all permitted uses of nitrate in curing of meats were stopped, the remaining uses of nitrate were restricted to a level of 200 parts per million, and the level of nitrite added in the curing of bacon was reduced to 150 parts per million and 200 parts per million in preparing other cured meat products. Regulations prohibiting the pre-mixing of nitrates and nitrite with other components of dry cures also were promulgated in 1975.

Until recently, concern about nitrite focused on the possibility that it could combine with other chemicals in foods and in the body to produce substances called nitrosamines, which are potent cancer-producing agents. A recent U.S. study by Professor Paul Newberne of the Massachusetts Institute of Technology has suggested that nitrite itself may produce cancer when fed in high doses to rats. Officials of the Health Protection Branch (HPB) are fully aware of the Newberne study and have been in close consultation with Dr. Newberne and with health officials in the United States and United Kingdom. A detailed examination of the Newberne study and of all other published information bearing on the safety of nitrite is being undertaken by HPB scientists.

HPB has had active programs of investigation on the safety of nitrites underway for several years. In a recently concluded long-term study conducted under contract for the Branch, rats were given diets that included 25 per cent cooked bacon made with or without nitrite throughout their lifespan. The incidence of cancer was unchanged in animals given the nitrite-cured bacon as compared to those receiving bacon without added nitrite. The results of this study provide added assurance on the safety of nitrite under practical conditions of use.

In considering appropriate action on nitrite, it must be kept in mind that its use is required to prevent growth in cured meats of *Clostridium botulinum*, a microorganism which causes botulism, a serious and often deadly disease. Nitrite also retards the growth of spoilage microorganisms and imparts a characteristic flavor and color to cured meats. To date, no suitable substitute for nitrite has been found. Thus, it is necessary to balance the essential value of nitrite in preventing botulism against the theoretical possibility that it may produce cancer, either directly or through the formation of nitrosamines. At present, if nitrite were not used, bacon, ham and other cured meat products as we know them would not be available to the public. The cooking times and temperatures necessary to ensure bacterial safety of canned meat products such as luncheon meats made without nitrite would render these products esthetically undesirable. All remaining smoked meat products would require storage at refrigeration temperatures.

Since no safe and effective substitute for nitrite is available, elimination of its use at this time would expose consumers of processed meats to the very real risk of botulism and would deprive consumers of the characteristic flavor and color of cured meats such as bacon and ham. "On the basis of a benefit to risk assessment, I have concluded that the elimination of nitrite would not be warranted," Miss Bégin reiterated.

In carrying forward its long-term policy to reduce

unnecessary use of nitrite, the HPB will continue to work closely with scientists in the Canadian meat industry and to closely monitor world experience with this substance. First priority will be given to investigations to determine whether the level of nitrite added in the curing of bacon can further be reduced without endangering the safety and esthetic desirability of the product. Additional investigations on the safety of nitrite and of possible substitutes are being planned jointly with health officials of the United States and the United Kingdom.

APPENDIX C

A Food Additive Opinion Survey

Beginning in 1979, the Health Protection Branch (HPB) of Health and Welfare Canada undertook a two-year project aimed at improving communication with consumers about food additives. The first phase of the project consisted of a survey of public attitudes towards these chemicals.

Between June and August of 1979, shoppers in 42 shopping malls in five cities—Vancouver, Winnipeg, Toronto, Montreal and Halifax—were asked by HPB workers to complete a 20-point questionnaire on food additives. Of those approached, 47 percent, or about 25,000 people, agreed to complete the questionnaire. It should be kept in mind that this method of surveying, though relatively inexpensive, does not produce a random sample (the cornerstone of a statistically valid survey). The sample is a "self-selected" one in which opinions about food additives may be stronger than in the population at large. Nevertheless, the results can give some indication of the level of concern within what *is* a large group of consumers.

The outcome of the survey portrayed a great deal of confusion and concern about additives among Canadian consumers:

- 87 percent of those surveyed were concerned about the possible health effects of eating additives.

- 70 percent felt that additives do not improve the quality of food.

- 68 percent felt that there is inadequate control of food additives. (Over one-quarter of those sampled were unclear as to whether there is any government regulation of these chemicals and whether food manufacturers have to test new additives before they are permitted in food.)

- 69 percent agreed that food colours are not a justifiable addition to food.

- 65 percent indicated a feeling that food labels do not provide a complete list of additives actually found in food.

- 76 percent said they make an effort to eat food containing fewer additives and 60 percent want additive-free food enough to say they are willing to pay more for it.

The Health and Welfare survey also found that there is considerable misunderstanding of what is included under the term "food additive." For example, 52 percent believed that pesticide residues are under the additive umbrella. In fact, the *Food and Drugs Act* does not define pesticides as such; the additive definition covers only food processing chemicals. In other words, a broader perception of food additives exists in the public mind than under federal law. This extra area of concern for incidental or environmental additives has not been adequately addressed in government programs of consumer education.

The survey revealed a heavy reliance for information on the mass media—newspapers, magazines, television and radio. Fewer people turn to government pamphlets and health food stores, and fewer still to dieticians, nutritionists, doctors and nurses. As the survey report put it, "The reliable professionals may not have been accessible or well-utilized by the public." (Books—such as *Additive Alert* —were not offered as a possible information source in the government questionnaire.)

One of the greatest concerns felt by the Health Protection Branch after receiving the survey results was consumers' misunderstanding of the benefits of additives. In a discussion of the survey in the *Canadian Institute of Food Science and Technology Journal,* the HPB surveyers noted that "the role of additives in food was not well known. Only a small percentage of the respondents recognized the potential benefits of additives. In fact, it was evident that many perceived additive ingestion as harmful. This seemed to override any notion as to the specific worthwhile functions and effects of these chemicals."

The second, follow-up phase of the HPB food additive project is aimed at addressing the concerns raised in the opinion survey, through distribution of federal publications at booths in shopping malls, presentations in schools, seminars for health professionals, and so on. A new arrival is HPB's *Food Additive Pocket Dictionary*, a 32-page index with an uncanny similarity to the one at the end of this book.

In the past couple of years, the Health Protection Branch has been criticized by some consumer activists, members of parliament and media representatives for alleged bias in favour of the food industry in public education campaigns on additives. In the news release accompanying publication of the additive opinion survey, Health and Welfare Minister Monique Bégin seemed to reveal such a bias: "Representatives of the food industry, after reviewing the survey results, have agreed to work towards better public understanding of the necessity for food additives in modern food processing. Through joint action it is hoped that communication with consumers can be improved in order to alleviate their expressed concerns."

Additives surfaced on the floor of the House of Commons in 1980. There were opposition charges that a new HPB slide show, *Alice in Additiveland*, to be used as a teaching aid in schools and elsewhere, was not only biased in favour of additives, but also sexist and patronizing in its overall tone. The slide show was recalled and modified slightly before being re-issued in 1981.

Publications relating to the opinion survey and HPB's educational efforts on food additives are listed in Chapter 7.

APPENDIX D

Twenty Most-Asked Questions About Food Additives... and Some Answers

1 *Just how appropriate is it to base the safety of human consumption of food additives on tests done on laboratory animals which are fed mega-doses of these chemicals? People aren't rats... and we don't consume 800 bottles of diet pop a day!*

True enough. There may be a wide margin of error between effects of additives on animals versus human beings. We may be more—or less—sensitive than test animals to these chemicals, or we may react in very different ways entirely. But at present, there are really no alternatives to high-dose animal studies:

(a) To do a scientifically valid study by feeding animals the same dose of an additive as people would consume would require too many animals and too much time. (For one thing, it would be prohibitively expensive.) We need answers to chemical safety questions now or next year, not in 1990.

(b) It's simply unethical to experiment directly on

human beings (although some people argue that this is precisely what is happening with regard to the suspicious additives already on the market). What must be done is to experiment with animal species that are as closely related to humans as possible, in "hopes" that health effects will be similar. Hence, tests on mammals such as rats, dogs or monkeys are more predictive (but also more expensive) than tests on bacteria, such as the Ames carcinogenicity test.

2 *What is your position on the safety of nitrites in prepared meats (bacon, ham, wieners, etc.)?*

The case of sodium nitrite as a preservative in cured meats is an unusual and complex one: Here, the risk of *not* using the additive—the possible contamination of the meat with the bacteria that cause botulism—may be as great as (some sources say greater than) the risk of using the chemical. The risk involves the combination of nitrite with food constituents called amines to form carcinogenic nitrosamines.

The debate over nitrites is fuelled by the following complications:

(a) Prepared meats are not the sole source of nitrite in our food. They comprise only 5 to 40 percent of our nitrite intake. The rest comes from "natural" sources, such as some vegetables and (believe it or not!) our own saliva. But cured meats represent the controllable part of our exposure to nitrite, so are worth a close look when it comes to cutting our nitrite intake.

(b) No really effective alternative chemical has

been found to replace nitrite. (Some 700 have been tested.)

In face of the above information, there is no easy answer to the nitrite question. The wisest course would be to reduce one's intake of prepared meats as much as "possible." (By way of example, concern might be raised if, in one day, a young child had bacon for breakfast, a hot dog for lunch and ham for dinner.) In addition, meat manufacturers can probably reduce the levels of nitrite they now use, while still retaining the preserving and colouring effects of the chemical. Finally, research into alternatives to nitrite use in cured meats must continue unabated.

3 *Does the dye used on orange skins get into the inside of the orange?*

The colouring agent used to turn orange skins a uniform deep orange colour is Citrus Red No. 2. By no means are all oranges treated this way. The skins of California oranges tend to achieve an orange colour on their own; it is the Florida oranges that are more likely to contain the dye.

Research to this point indicates that the dye sits tight in the skin of the orange; the juicy part is left untouched. This fact is the basis for permitting the use of Citrus Red No. 2 on oranges sold in Canada, even though the Food and Agriculture Organization and the World Health Organization (the two United Nations agencies which make recommendations to national governments on food additive use) advise that this dye not be used as a "direct" food additive. (The dye has been linked to cancer and other health effects in laboratory animals.) In other words, adding colour to orange skins is considered an "indirect" additive, since generally the skin is discarded and the edible part of the orange has no direct addition of colour made to it.

However, sometimes we *do* eat orange peel. It may be used in marmalade, in candied rind, in recipes calling for grated orange rind, and so on. Also, if you peel oranges with your teeth, you'll inadvertently consume a small amount of the dye.

There is little, if any, justification for the continued use of Citrus Red No. 2 on orange skins. Here is a prime example of a food additive of highly questionable safety being used for a totally cosmetic purpose. While waiting for a ban on Citrus Red No. 2, try using lemon instead of orange rind in cooking, since the flavour is similar. No added colour is permitted on lemons (or on any other citrus fruits besides oranges.)

4 *Is colour permitted in fresh meat?*

Absolutely not. Any meat wholesaler or retailer who has been found to be tampering with the colour of unprocessed meat, usually with the intention of making the meat look fresher than it really is, is prosecuted by federal health authorities. By contrast, producers of processed meats such as ham, wierners, bacon and so on, may use additives such as sodium nitrite, which both preserve the meat and bring out a pinkish colour, without actually being colouring agents themselves.

5 *What is the difference between 'brown bread' and 'whole wheat bread'?*

Any bread can be called brown bread, regardless of the whole wheat flour content. (It helps, though, if it looks brown too.) In fact, brown bread may have *no* whole wheat flour at all! The bread looks like whole wheat because it has added colouring. The colouring agent commonly used is caramel, an additive of questionable safety. On the other hand, any bread claiming to be whole wheat bread must, under the *Food and Drugs Act*, contain at least 60 percent whole wheat flour, the remainder being white flour. (Caramel colour may be used even in these breads, however.)

A pre-packaged brown bread made without any whole wheat flour must declare this fact on the label. Where whole wheat flour *is* used, the percentage used must be stated on the label. Brown bread is the only food in Canada for which the law requires the colour to be listed by name; caramel, molasses, or both (whichever is/are used) must be on the label.

Be particularly on the lookout for coloured bread in bakeries where bread is sold without labels declaring the bread's ingredients. Colour is used more frequently there than in bread sold in supermarkets and convenience stores; pre-packaged breads in those stores must list ingredients, and colour is seldom one of them.

Rye bread also is very often coloured. You can be sure that any rye bread that looks like chocolate cake has added colour!

6 *Is colour allowed on apples?*

No. However, what often makes Red Delicious apples appear deliciously red is the shine achieved by applying a thin coating of paraffin wax. (The wax also helps preserve the apple to a small extent.) A vigorous scrubbing should remove this coating which, some sources say, may affect the digestive system.

7 *Why do butter wrappers state that the butter 'may contain colour'? Don't the dairies know whether or not they put in colour?!*

The natural colour of butter varies with the time of year. In the summer, the cattle are grazing in open pasture. Their butter is the characteristic yellow colour because of the presence of carotene pigments in their diet. By contast, winter butter is much paler because the cattle feed in that season is not as high in carotene. So it is primarily in the winter that extra colour is added to butter. To avoid having to change labels with the change in seasons, the dairies cover both possibilities by stating that the butter "may contain colour."

Although the most commonly used colour, annatto, is from a natural source and is purportedly non-toxic, some thirty other colours are allowed, including some synthetic ones of questionable safety (such as caramel, amaranth and tartrazine). A shortcoming in our food labelling laws (see Chapter 4) means that without contacting the dairy directly, we can't be sure which colour is being used, since colours need not be given by name on labels.

It is almost impossible to find, in the commercial marketplace, butter that is uncoloured in all seasons. We're told by the dairy people that consumers prefer butter that is consistently yellow. Do you? Butter can be purchased in both salted and unsalted forms; why not coloured and uncoloured as well? It can be argued that such a basic, relatively unprocessed food as butter should be available without *any* chemical additives, all year round.

8 *We hear a lot about the effects of food additives, especially artificial colours, on children diagnosed as hyperactive (hyperkinetic). In the late 1970s, there was considerable support for the diet developed for hyperactive children by the American allergist and pediatrician Ben Feingold (described briefly in Chapter 6). How much support does Feingold's diet theory have now?*

Though many parents of hyperactive children believe strongly in the benefits of the Feingold diet, it has not stood up very well in rigorous, clinical studies of its effectiveness. There appears to be a small sub-group of hyperactive children who are, indeed, helped by a diet that eliminates many food additives.

But scientific studies in the past five years have determined that the improvement of many hyperactive children on the Feingold diet may be due to factors other than the chemical composition of their food. For example, the special attention given to a hyperactive child in the administration of the Feingold diet may have as much effect on his/her behaviour as do the additives, if not more effect.

The relationship between diet and hyperactivity is a complex one. Those wishing to pursue it further are urged to read the book by C. Keith Connors, *Food Additives and Hyperactive Children* and the article in the journal *Pediatrics* by Stare, Whelan and Sheridan, both listed in Chapter 7.

9 *What colour additives are used in drugs?*

Many of the colouring agents used in both prescription and over-the-counter medications are the same ones used in foods. As is the case for colourings in foods, colours in drugs are not given by name at the consumer level.

The use of dyes in drugs presents an entirely different problem from their use in foods. The consumer has much less choice over what medication he/she takes than what food he/she eats. In other words, it's much more difficult to avoid added colours in drugs. But in some cases, alternative formulations of the same drug may be available without added colour. Consult your physician or pharmacist.

10 *Are baby foods loaded with additives?*

In recent years, many consumers, nutritionists and pediatricians have been critical of certain features of commercially prepared baby foods. This criticism has prompted both voluntary reformulation of these products by manufacturers and government restrictions on the use of certain chemicals and ingredients.

Under the *Food and Drugs Act*, the use of food additives is forbidden in food intended for consumption by infants under one year of age, with the following exceptions: ascorbic acid, used as an antioxidant in dry cereals containing banana; soyabean lecithin used in rice cereals, to prevent sticking during manufacturing and to enhance flavour; and citric acid, which shortens the heating process, thereby helping to maintain the food's flavour and colour.

Monosodium glutamate (MSG) is not classified

as a food additive in Canada, so doesn't fall under the above restrictions. However, Canadian baby food manufacturers voluntarily removed MSG from their products in 1969, due to both adverse publicity about MSG's health effects and lack of evidence to justify its inclusion in infant foods.

Likewise, modified starches are not classified as food additives, so don't fall under the above restrictions. Yet some 23 chemicals are permitted as starch modifying agents. Parents wishing to avoid feeding additives to their babies should therefore watch for the presence of modified starch.

Other concerns about commercial baby foods relate to the amount of salt and sugar, two substances not included as food additives under Canadian law.

11 *Are any additives permitted in milk?*

On the surface, no. Vitamins A and D are added, but these are not included under the Canadian definition of food additives. However, preparations of these fat-soluble vitamins for use in milk are allowed to contain the antioxidant preservatives butylated hydroxyanisole (BHA) and butylated hydroxytoluene (BHT). As indicated on page 50, food labels remain "silent" when it comes to additives used in the preparation of some food ingredients, including vitamins. That is, the ingredient is listed on the label (cocoa, flour, vitamin A, etc.), but the constituents of the ingredient are not.

Check with your local dairy to determine if the vitamin preparations it uses contain BHT and/or BHA.

12 *How can I possibly avoid all the potentially*

harmful food additives? It seems that there are additives in everything!

Not so. Let's not be so presumptuous! With some exceptions (see Chapter Four), a careful reading of each food label you encounter will indicate foods with and without additives. Furthermore, it's unnecessary to reject a food simply because there is a list of additives on the label. The majority of additives are widely considered to be safe.

If a generalization can be made about the types of foods that contain additives, it would be this: The more processed the food, the heavier the content of additives. Convenience foods (from instant breakfasts to cake mixes, snack foods to jelly desserts) have more chemicals than basic foods (butter, milk, flour, etc.).

13 *Without resort to the food additive index at the back of* Additive Alert, *the lists of additives on food packages giving complex chemical names are next to useless to the average consumer. Isn't there a way in which the information could be made more accessible?*

One option would be to state in parentheses, after each additive on a food label, the function of the additive. Some manufacturers already do this for some of their products, although there is no legal requirement to do so. For example, sometimes one encounters "BHT (to maintain freshness)," a rather endearing phrase meaning "preservative."

Of course, a food label would never indicate which additives are of questionable safety, the other feature of this book's index.

14 *I would like to switch to decaffeinated coffee because of the numerous reports of the effects of caffeine on the nervous system and now the risk of birth defects in children of mothers who have been heavy coffee drinkers. But I've heard some unsavoury things about the chemicals used to decaffeinate coffee. Help! Which risk is greater, the caffeine or the decaffeinating chemicals?*

The extraction solvents that have been used to coax caffeine out of coffee include methylene chloride (dichloromethane) and trichloroethylene. Under current Canadian law, the only solvent allowed for decaffeinating coffee is methylene chloride; trichloroethylene was de-listed (banned) in 1977. The solvent does not have to be listed on coffee jars or bags, but that doesn't mean that solvent residues aren't permitted. Regulations under the *Food and Drugs Act* allow methylene chloride to remain in both decaffeinated coffee beans and decaffeinated instant coffee at a level of 10 parts per million (ppm).

Though methylene chloride is not as suspect in terms of toxicity as is its predecessor, trichlorethylene, it does not have a perfectly clean bill of health. Both are chlorinated hydrocarbons, related chemically to numerous toxic, sometimes carcinogenic, substances (DDT, for one).

It has been argued that the risk of imbibing small amounts of solvents along with your decaffeinated coffee is very small. For example, one would have to drink 50 *million* cups of decaffeinated coffee per day over one's whole lifetime to achieve the dosage level of trichlorethylene found to have health effects on test animals. Judging from the large body of information on the toxic effects of caffeine at the levels actually consumed by human coffee drinkers, it would seem that if you want to drink coffee, the decaffeinated kind is probably the lesser of two evils.

15 *How do food processing additives fit into the whole topic of food quality, which includes concerns about nutrition, pesticides and so on?*

The various risks involved in eating are as follows (*not* necessarily in order of importance): improper nutrition, food processing additives, pesticide residues, drug residues, mycotoxins (poisonous moulds on some foods), pollutants from air and water, toxic chemicals occurring naturally in food crops, and food poisoning by bacteria. These risks are outlined in more detail in Chapter 3 of *The Invisible Additives*, Pollution Probe's handbook on environmental contaminants in food.

It is very difficult to assign priorities to these risks. Each interest group—government or industry officials, independent scientists, public interest and consumer advocates—looks at food risks differently.

16 *I'm on a low-sodium diet, so I have to restrict my salt intake. Are there food additives that should be avoided as well?*

Yes. Any food additive that contains sodium would be of concern to people on low-sodium diets. These include the commonly used flavour enhancer monosodium glutamate (MSG) and the preservatives sodium nitrite and sodium benzoate. In fact, any additive in the index at the back of this book that contains the word "sodium" is of relevance to those needing to reduce sodium intake. Consult your physician or dietician for further guidance.

17 *What is the justification for banning saccharin from foods yet still allowing it to be used in the so-called "table-top sweeteners"?*

Saccharin was banned from use in food in Canada in 1977, after Canadian studies linked it to bladder cancer in male rats. There have been many other laboratory reports that have found *no* problems with saccharin, and the artificial sweetener is still permitted (on a temporary basis) in the United States.

Removing saccharin from food while continuing to permit its sale as a table-top sweetener can be rationalized on two grounds:

(a) The use of saccharin in food products was a broad use covering numerous foods, from diet soft drinks to chewing gum. Only careful label-reading would determine the presence of saccharin. Now, saccharin use is restricted to sweeteners deliberately added by the consumer, at home, to a restricted group of foods, such as coffee and tea.

(b) Many diabetics rely on saccharin as a sugar substitute. It is the only non-caloric sweetener available. Banning saccharin altogether, it has been argued, would be unfair to diabetics. Also, saccharin is valued by people with serious problems of overweight, although some research indicates that the benefits may be only perceived rather than real.

There is currently a proposal in the hands of the federal health agencies in both the United States and Canada to allow the use in foods of aspartame, a low-calorie (not no-calorie) sweetener. Thousands of pages of evidence supporting its safety have been filed, but the jury is still out in both countries.

18 *If you could change one Canadian law relating to food additives, what would it be?*

The change would be a labelling one—the listing of added colours *by specific name*. There is no solid justification for exempting colours from specific declaration on food labels. Some of the most prevalent allergies to individual food additives are to colours, and consumers sensitive to only certain colours should not have to avoid *all* foods with "colour" simply because that's all the labels tell them.

The United States government is taking a step in the direction of better disclosure of colours on food labels. The U.S. Food and Drug Administration (F.D.A.) estimates that as many as 100,000 Americans are allergic to the yellow colour tartrazine (U.S. Yellow Dye No. 5). So, effective July 1, 1981, all foods containing tartrazine must list it specifically on food labels. But why stop at tartrazine, in the U.S. *or* Canada? Let's see *all* colours labelled by name.

Discussions on food colour labelling are currently underway between Health and Welfare Canada and Consumer and Corporate Affairs Canada. A public position on the subject has yet to be released, but appears to be forthcoming.

19 *Even if all potentially toxic chemicals in food were removed, we'd still be breathing polluted air and drinking polluted water. So what good does it do to solve only part of the environmental health problem?*

Reducing our exposure to toxic chemicals *however* possible is the name of the game. We'll likely never achieve "zero risk" from chemicals in the environment, but that's no reason to stop trying to minimize our exposure to these chemicals by whatever means they enter our bodies. Efforts to rid our diet of harmful substances must be made as part of the broader process of cleaning up the environment generally.

20 *It seems that everything causes cancer!*

Not true. While the chemicals that *do* cause cancer have captured a lot of attention in recent years, many more have no links with tumour development whatsoever. According to the United States Environmental Protection Agency (E.P.A.), of the roughly 7,000 chemicals that have been tested for carcinogenicity (ability to induce cancer), all but about 500, or about 7 percent, have gotten a clean bill of health in this regard.

We must remember, however, that there are plenty of health effects other than cancer that may have food additives at their source. The guide to suspicious additives in Chapter Three bears out this notion.

Two readable sources of information on chemicals and cancer are the E.P.A.'s pamphlet entitled *This Rat Died in a Cancer Lab to Save Lives* and a booklet by the Center for Science in the Public Interest called *Does Everything Cause Cancer?* For a complete, referenced list of all the chemicals that cause cancer, in animals and/or humans (if known), contact the Carcinogen Information Program in St. Louis, Missouri. (For details on these sources, see Chapter Seven.)

APPENDIX E

Labelling Foods "Natural": Sense and Nonsense

This appendix expands on and updates the section of Chapter Four (pages 53-54) that covers the use of words like "natural" and "pure" on food labels.

The trend in the food industry toward willy-nilly labelling of food as "natural," "wholesome" and/or "pure" continues unabated, at the expense of the consumer who believes that he/she is buying a completely additive-free product.

In December 1979, *New York Times* writer Jane Brody put the problem this way: "'Natural' is simply the food industry's way of evading consumer distrust of factory-made foods; sometimes the very same artificial foods that the word natural is used to describe. 'Natural' means whatever the manufacturer chooses it to mean, and that can be very different from what the consumer thinks it means."

The Consumers' Association of Canada is currently interested in surveying consumer (mis)understanding of what "natural" means on a food labels, but at present, no Canadian studies on the subject have been published. However, a couple of U.S. reports are probably applicable to the Canadian scene:

- A survey taken by the Consumer Response Corporation revealed that the word "natural" was the most convincing claim to put on a food label. It outranked freshness, value, convenience and flavour. Forty-two percent of consumers surveyed believed that products touted as "natural" had no harmful effects and were safer and healthier than other food products. There is, of course, no evidence to support such assumptions.

- A study by the U.S. government's Federal Trade Commission found that 63 percent of those surveyed agreed that natural foods are more nutritious than other foods and 47 percent indicated a willingness to pay 10 percent more for a food that is labelled "natural."

The inescapable conclusion is that consumers generally believe that "natural" means "no additives," when in fact, without a legal definition of "natural," the word means no such thing. One could go so far as to say that "natural" as it now stands is an altogether useless and misleading word to put on food labels.

Speaking of legalities... the word "pure" on food labels has a long legal history in Canada. A food that is unadulterated is "pure"; there is *no* connection between "pure" and absence of food additives, even though consumers aften make such a connection and some food advertisers imply it. No attempt is being made by Consumer and Corporate Affairs Canada (CCAC) to redefine "pure" or restrict the use of the word on food labels.

However, for CCAC, the word "natural" is another kettle of fish. In April 1981, Kathleen Francoeur Hendriks, Assistant Deputy Minister in charge of Consumer Affairs at CCAC, stated the following: "I can confirm that the proposed communiqué on the use of the term 'natural' to describe foods or their ingredients, is being actively worked on and we anticipate its release in the next few months. This communiqué will set forth options, including possible legislative action, to control the use of the term."

Readers wishing to obtain this communiqué on "natural" labels and to contribute their comments on the subject should contact Consumer and Corporate Affairs (see address on page 57).

Now a few words about the perceived infallibility of health food stores when it comes to the stocking of additive-free foods. Though proprietors of a good many health food stores sincerely try to stock no-additive products, *caveat emptor* (let the buyer beware) applies here as in any other store. Notes Merilyn Mohr in *Harrowsmith* magazine's *The Canadian Whole Food Book:* "To assume that all the goods in a health food store are wholesome and pristine is as naive as to assume that all supermarket products are overprocessed, chemicalized parodies of real food."

Even careful label-reading, the usual safeguard, may not be protection enough. Consumer confidence in the insurance value of reading food labels to ascertain additive content was shaken by research performed for Montreal television station CFCF in 1979. Several products sold in health food stores, all bearing additive-free labels, were found to contain chemical preservatives. For example, one brand of peanut butter contained a high level of BHT in the oil on top of the peanut butter, despite the label's claim that only peanuts were used in production of the spread. Other offending products included vegetable oils, potato chips, margarines and breads.

Fortunately, the preservatives were present at levels below the maximums set out under the *Food and Drugs Act.* But the real issue here is deceptive labelling. In reports of the CFCF research in *The Whig-Standard* (Kingston, Ontario), a spokesperson for Consumer and Corporate Affairs Canada admitted that the department lacks the money and people to regularly inspect the products of manufacturers in the health food sector of the food industry. As one CCAC source put it, the health food industry "makes more outward claims" about its products than other sectors and "lends itself to the fast-buck market in some cases. It's a hell of a temptation to pass off ordinary food as health food."

The extent to which this type of fraud occurs is unknown. Let's hope it's the exception rather than the rule, and that, in general, the integrity of health food manufacturers can be relied upon.

For a discussions of the labelling of fresh produce as "organically grown" (another area where legal definition is lacking), see Chapter 6 of Pollution Probe's *The Invisible Additives*.

A Pollution Probe Synopsis of Other Food Issues

The issue of processing additives in our food is a complex and important one. We certainly *are* what we eat! Many other factors influence how well we eat. This section opens the door to those issues.

Agricultural Chemicals

Residues of pesticides used on crops and drugs used in livestock are "invisible" additives. They do not appear on food labels; their presence in food that reaches the dinner plate is inconsistent and unplanned.

Pesticides include insecticides, herbicides (weedkillers) and fungicides. Drugs used in animal production include antibiotics (such as penicillin, tetracycline and sulfonamides) and, to a lesser extent, hormones.

We must be as concerned about pesticides and drugs in our food as we are about intentional food additives, if not more so. After all, since pesticides are meant to kill and drugs exert powerful biological effects, these chemicals are unlikely to be the most benign additives to our food.

For further information on agricultural chemicals in food (as well as other "invisible" additives such as aflatoxin, PCBs and dioxin), see:

PIM, LINDA R. *The Invisible Additives: Environmental Contaminants in Our Food.* Toronto: Doubleday Canada, 1981. (A Project of Pollution Probe)

Nutrition

Merely eliminating unnecessary and potentially harmful food additives from the diet is no guarantee that a healthful eating pattern will result. We may be well-fed, but many of us are undernourished! In other words, we may be getting enough food (and, in many cases, too much), but that food might have insufficient amounts of vitamins and minerals, for example. What about balanced meals, fibre, nutritional supplements and restricted diets? What about salt, sugar and vegetarians?

For further information on nutrition, see:

DOYLE, RODGER P. and REDDING, JAMES L. *The Complete Food Handbook.* 3rd. edition. New York: Grove Press, 1979.

Eating in America: Dietary Goals for the United States. Report of the Select Committee on Nutrition and Human Needs, U.S. Senate (George McGovern, Chairman). Cambridge, Mass.: The MIT Press, 1977.

FREMES, RUTH and SABRY, ZAK. *Nutriscore: The Rate-Yourself Plan for Better Nutrition.* Toronto: Methuen, 1976.

GOLDBECK, NIKKI and DAVID. *The Supermarket Handbook: Access to Whole Foods.* Revised and Expanded Edition. New York: New American Library (Signet), 1976.

JACOBSON, MICHAEL F. *Nutrition Scoreboard: Your Guide to Better Eating.* Washington. D.C.: Avon Books, 1975. (Center for Science in the Public Interest)

Ontario Dietetic Association and Ontario Hospital Association. *The Nuts and Bolts of Nutrition.* Toronto: Ontario Hospital Association, 1980. (Available for $4.95 by writing to: Dietetic Services, Ontario Hospital Association, 150 Ferrand Drive, Don Mills, Ontario, M3C 1H6)

Food Packaging Chemicals

No person shall sell any food in a package that may yield to its contents any substance that may be injurious to the health of the consumer of the food.

Section B.23.001 of the *Food and Drug Regulations*

Sometimes BHT is added to food packaging materials with the intention that the preservative will migrate into the food and retard spoilage. On the other hand, undesirable but also unintentional additives may migrate into food, too. In the early 1970s, polychlorinated biphenyls (PCBs) were appearing in the cardboard used to package food products. Also, the increasing use of plastics as food packaging materials has prompted studies of the toxicity of some plastics such as polyvinyl chloride (PVC), polystyrene (Styrofoam) and acrylonitrile (AN). The best known case of a possible health hazard from food packages is the transfer of lead from cans into food. Of particular concern are high-acid goods (such as tomato and fruit juices) and baby foods.

For more information on food packaging chemicals, see:

PIM, LINDA R. *The Invisible Additives: Environmental Contaminants in Our Food*. Toronto: Doubleday Canada, 1981.

Over-Packaging of Food

Packaging in necessary; over-packaging is not! You don't carry home a pound of cheese in the palm of your hand, but you'd do fine without a plastic wrapping around that fresh coconut! You'd also eat just as well if soup mixes, cheese slices, puddings and fruit juices weren't packaged individually; if fresh vegetables weren't wrapped up in plastic and cardboard; if margarine weren't clothed in three layers of packaging; and so on.

A hefty percentage of residential garbage is made up of packaging materials (for food and other products). We could eliminate the wastage involved if we did away with the extra layers. Paring down packaging constitutes one of the three Rs of cutting the garbage glut—*r*educing garbage by eliminating packaging frills (send the package back to the company president! Complain that it's not needed!); *re*-using glass and plastic containers; and *r*ecycling whatever cannot be reduced or re-used.

The Food Chain

What are the components of the food system in Canada? What forces come into play between the grower at one end and the eater at the other?

For information on the Canadian food chain, see:

The Land of Milk and Money: The National Report of the

People's Food Commission. Kitchener, Ontario: Between the Lines, 1980.

National Farmers Union. *Nature Feeds Us: The Food System from Soil to Table.* Saskatoon: 1976. (Available from: NFU, 250C Second Avenue South, Saskatoon, Saskatchewan, S7K 2M1)

STEWART, WALTER. *Hard to Swallow: Why Food Prices Keep Rising and What Can Be Done About It.* Toronto: Macmillan of Canada, 1974.

WARNOCK, JOHN W. *Profit Hungry: The Food Industry in Canada.* Vancouver: New Star Books, 1978.

The Global Food Supply

Different authors blame different culprits in the battle over world hunger. Some, such as George, Lappé and Collins (below) say there *is* enough food to go around on Planet Earth. They maintain that people are starving because of the way food is distributed globally, the conversion of food grains into meat, and the cultivation of luxury food and non-food crops on good land. Other authors, such as Brown (below), believe that bad weather, poor soil management and over-population are to blame.

For more information on the world food problem, see:

BROWN, LESTER. *The Twenty Ninth Day: Accommodating Human Needs and Numbers to the Earth's Resources.* New York: W.W. Norton, 1978.

GEORGE, SUSAN. *How the Other Half Dies: The Real Reasons for World Hunger.* Penguin, 1977.

LAPPE, FRANCES MOORE and COLLINS, JOSEPH. *Food First: Beyond the Myth of Scarcity.* Boston: Houghton Mifflin, 1977.

The Food Additive Index

This index lists all the additives permitted in food in Canada, excluding specific flavouring compounds (which are not regulated by law). After each additive is given the function(s) served by that additive. Those additives considered to be of questionable safety are printed in **bold type.**

The code for additive functions is as follows:

A	Anti-caking agents
B	Bleaching, maturing and dough conditioning agents
C	Colours
E	Extraction (carrier) solvents
EN	Food enzymes
F	Flavours
FE	Flavour enhancers
G	Glazing and polishing agents
M	Starch modifying agents
P	Preservatives
pH	Acid/base balancing additives
S	Sequestering agents

T	Texture agents (emulsifiers, stabilizers, gelling and thickening agents)
V	Vitamin, mineral or other nutrient supplements (shown in parentheses)
X	Firming agents
Y	Yeast foods
Z	Miscellaneous additives (various purposes)

Acacia gum (gum arabic)	T, G
Acetic acid	pH, P
Acetic anhydride	M
Acetone	E
Acetone peroxide	B
Acetylated monoglycerides	T, G, Z
Acetylated tartaric acid esters of Mono- and Diglycerides	T
Adipic acid	pH, M
Agar-agar	T
Algin	T
Alginic acid	T
Alkanet	C
Alpha amylase bacillus subtilis enzyme	B
Alum (or **potassium aluminum sulphate**)	X, Z, pH
Aluminum metal	C
Aluminum sulphate	X, Z, M
Amaranth (U.S. Red Dye No. 2)	C
Ammonium alginate	T
Ammonium aluminum sulphate	X, pH

Ammonium bicarbonate	pH
Ammonium carbonate	pH
Ammonium carrageenan	T
Ammonium chloride	Y
Ammonium citrate, mono- and dibasic	pH, S
Ammonium furcelleran	T
Ammonium hydroxide	pH
Ammonium persulphate	B, Z
Ammonium phosphate, mono- and dibasic	pH, Y
Ammonium salt of phosphorylated glyceride	T
Ammonium sulphate	Y
Annatto	C
Anthocyanins	C
β-Apo-8'-carotenal	C
Arabinogalactin	T
Artificial colours	C
Artificial flavours	F
Ascorbic acid	B, P, V
Ascorbyl palmitate	P
Ascorbyl stearate	P
Aspergillus flavus oryzae enzyme	B
Aspergillus niger enzyme	B
Azodicarbonamide	B
BHA (butylated hydroxyanisole)	P
BHT (butylated hydroxytoluene)	P
Baker's yeast glycan	T
Beeswax	G, Z
Beet red	C

Benzoic Acid	P
Benzoyl Peroxide	B
Benzyl alcohol	E
Bicarbonate of soda (or sodium bicarbonate)	Z, pH, M
(Biotin)	V
Brilliant blue FCF (U.S. Blue Dye No.1)	C
Bromelain	EN
Brominated vegetable oil	Z, FE
Butylated hydroxyanisole (BHA)	P
Butylated hydroxytoluene (BHT)	P
1, 3-butylene glycol	E
Caffeine	Z, FE
Caffeine citrate	Z
Calcium acetate	pH
Calcium alginate	T
Calcium aluminum silicate	A
Calcium ascorbate	P
Calcium carbonate	T, Z, pH, Y
Calcium carrageenan	T
Calcium chloride	X, pH, Y
Calcium citrate	T, X, pH, S, Y
Calcium disodium EDTA	S
Calcium fumarate	pH
Calcium furcelleran	T
Calcium gluconate	T, X, pH
Calcium glycerophosphate	T
Calcium hydroxide	pH
Calcium hypophosphite	T
Calcium iodate	B

Calcium lactate	pH, Y
Calcium oxide	pH
Calcium peroxide	B
Calcium phosphate, monobasic	X, pH, S, Y
Calcium phosphate, dibasic	T, X, Z, pH, Y
Calcium phosphate, tribasic (or tricalcium phosphate)	A, T, Z, pH, S,
Calcium phytate	S
Calcium propionate	P
Calcium silicate	A, Z
Calcium sorbate	P
Calcium stearate	A, Z
Calcium stearoyl-2-lactylate	B, Z
Calcium sulphate	T, X, Z, pH, Y
Calcium tartrate	T
Candelilla wax	G
Canthaxanthin	C
Caramel	C
Carbohydrase	EN
Carbon black	C
Carbon dioxide	Z
Carboxymethyl cellulose	T
Carnauba wax	G
Carob bean gum (or locust bean gum)	T
Carotene	C
Carrageenan	T
Castor Oil	Z, E
Catalase, from aspergillus	EN
Cellulase, from aspergillus niger group	EN

Cellulose, microcrystalline (or
    microcrystalline cellulose)   Z

Cellulose gum   T

Charcoal   C

Chlorine   B

Chlorine dioxide   B

Chloropentafluoroethane   Z

Chlorophyll   C

Citric Acid $\bar{Z}$, p$\bar{H}$, $\bar{P}$, $\hat{S}$

Citrus red no. 2   C

Cochineal   C

Colour. *See* C-letter-coded additives

Copper gluconate   Z

Cream of tartar   pH

(Cyanocobalamin [or vitamin B 12])   V

l-cysteine [hydrochloride]   B

Diammonium citrate
    (or ammonium citrate, dibasic)   pH, S

Diammonium phosphate
    (or ammonium phosphate, dibasic)   pH, Y

1,2-dichloroethane
    (or ethylene dichloride)   E

Dicalcium phosphate
    (or calcium phosphate, dibasic)   T, X, Z, pH, Y

Dichloromethane (or **methylene
    dichloride**)   E

Dimethylpolysiloxane formulations   Z

Dioctylsodium sulfo-succinate   Z

Dipotassium phosphate
    (or potassium phosphate, dibasic)   T, pH, Y

Disodium ethylenediaminetetraacetate
    (or **disodium EDTA**)   S
Disodium guanylate   FE
Disodium inosinate   FE
Disodium phosphate
    (or sodium phosphate, dibasic)   T, Z, pH, S

Epichlorohydrin   M
Erythorbic acid (or iso-ascorbic acid)   P
Erythrosine   C
Ethanol (or ethyl alcohol)   E
Ethyl acetate   E
Ethyl alcohol (or ethanol)   E
Ethyl β-Apo-8'-carotenate   C
Ethylenediaminetetraacetate (or
    EDTA)   S
Ethylene dichloride (or 1, 2-
    dichloroethane)   E
Ethylene oxide   Z

Fast green FCF   C
Ferrous gluconate   Z
Ficin   EN
Flavours   F
(Folic acid)   V
Fumaric acid   pH
Furcelleran   T

Gamma radiation from cobalt 60
    source   Z
Gelatin   T
Gluconic acid   T
Glucono delta lactone   Z, pH

Glucose oxidase-catalase	EN
Glycerin (or glycerol)	E, Z
Glycerol (or glycerin)	E, Z
Glyceryl diacetate	E
Glyceryl mono acetate (or monoacetin)	Z
Glyceryl triacetate (or triacetin)	Z, E
Glyceryl tributyrate (or tributyrin)	E
Glycine	S
Guaiac gum (or gum guaicum)	T, G
Gum guaicum (or guaiac gum)	T, G
Guar gum	T
Gum arabic (or acacia gum)	T, G
Gum benzoin	G
Hexane	E
(Histidine)	V
Hydrochloric acid	pH, M
Hydrogen peroxide	M
Hydrolyzed vegetable protein (contains **MSG**)	FE
Hydroxylated lecithin	T
Hydroxypropyl cellulose	T
Hydroxypropyl methylcellulose	T
(Iodine)	V
Indigotine	C
Invertase	EN
Irish moss gelose	T
(Iron, reduced)	V
Iron oxide	C

Iso-ascorbic acid (or erythorbic acid)	P
Isobutane	Z
(Isoleucine)	V
Isopropanol (or isopropyl alcohol)	E
Isopropyl alcohol (or isopropanol)	E
Karaya gum	T
Lactic acid	pH
Lactylated mono- and diglycerides	T
Lactylic esters of fatty acids	T, Z
Lanolin	Z
Lecithin	T, Z, P
Lecithin citrate	P
(Leucine)	V
Lipase	EN
Locust bean gum (or carob bean-gum)	T
(Lysine)	V
MSG (monosodium glutamate)	FE
Magnesium aluminum silicate	Z
Magnesium carbonate	A, Z, pH
Magnesium citrate	pH
Magnesium fumarate	pH
Magnesium hydroxide	pH
Magnesium oxide	A, pH
Magnesium silicate	A, G, Z
Magnesium stearate	A, Z
Magnesium sulphate	pH, M
Malic acid	pH
Maltol	FE
Manganese sulphate	Y

Mannitol — Z
(Methionine) — V
Methanol (or methyl alcohol) — E
Methyl alcohol (or methanol) — E
Methylcellulose — T
Methyl ethyl cellulose — T, Z
Methyl-p-hydroxybenzoate (or methyl paraben) — P
Methyl paraben (or methyl-p-hydroxybenzoate) — P
Methylene chloride (or **dichloromethane**) — E
Microcrystalline cellulose (or cellulose, microcrystalline) — Z
Milk-coagulating enzyme from mucor miehei — EN
Milk-coagulating enzyme from mucor pusillus lindt — EN
Mineral oil — G, Z
Modified starch. *See* M-letter-coded additives
Monoacetin (or glyceryl monoacetate) — Z
Mono- and diglycerides — T, Z
Monoglyceride citrate — P, E
Monoisopropyl citrate — P
Monoammonium glutamate — FE
Monopotassium glutamate — FE
Monosodium glutamate (or MSG) — FE

Natural colours — C
Natural flavours — F
(Niacin) — V

(Niacinamide)	V
Nitrate (sodium nitrate, potassium nitrate)	P
Nitric acid	M
Nitrite (sodium nitrite, potassium nitrite)	P
Nitrogen	Z
2-nitropropane	E
Nitrous oxide	Z
Oat gum	T
Octenyl succinic anhydride	M
Octafluorocyclobutane	Z
Orchil	C
Oxystearin	Z
Ozone	Z
Pancreas extract	Z
Pancreatin	EN
(d-pantothenic acid)	V
Papain	EN
Paprika	C
Paraffin wax	Z
Pectin	T
Pectinase	EN
Pepsin	EN
Peracetic acid	M
Petrolatum	G, Z
(Phenylalanine)	V
Phosphoric acid	pH, S, Y
Phosphorus oxychloride	M
Polyglycerol esters of fatty acids	T

Polyglycerol esters of interesterified
    castor oil fatty acids   T

Polyoxyethylene (20) sorbitan
    monooleate (or polysorbate 80)   T

Polyoxyethylene (20) sorbitan
    monostearate (or polysorbate 60)   T

Polyoxyethylene (8) stearate   T

Polysorbate 60 (or polyoxyethylene
    [20] sorbitan monostearate)   T

Polysorbate 80 (or polyoxyethylene
    [20] sorbitan monooleate)   T

Polyvinylpyrrolidone   Z

Ponceau SX (U.S. Red Dye No. 4)   C

Potassium acid tartrate (or potassium
    bitartrate)   pH

Potassium alginate   T

Potassium aluminum sulphate (or **alum**)   X, Z, pH

Potassium bisulphite   P

Potassium bitartrate (or potassium
    acid tartrate)   pH

Potassium bromate   B

Potassium carbonate   pH

Potassium carrageenan   T

Potassium chloride   T, pH, Y

Potassium citrate   T, pH

Potassium fumarate   pH

Potassium furcelleran   T

Potassium hydroxide   pH

Potassium iodate   B

Potassium metabisulphite   P

Potassium nitrate   P

Potassium nitrite   P

Potassium permanganate   M

Potassium persulphate   B

Potassium phosphate, monobasic (or
     potassium phosphate)   S, Y

Potassium phosphate, dibasic (or
     dipotassium phosphate)   T, pH, Y

Potassium pyrophosphate, tetrabasic
     (or potassium pyrophosphate)   S

Potassium sorbate   P

Potassium stearate   Z

Potassium sulphate   pH

Potassium tartrate   pH

Preservatives. *See* P-letter-coded
     additives

Propane   Z

1, 2-propanediol (or **propylene glycol**)   A, Z, E

Propionic acid   P

Propyl gallate   P

Propylene glycol (or **1, 2-propanediol**)   A, Z, E

Propylene glycol alginate   T

Propylene glycol ester of
     methylcellulose   T

Propylene glycol mono fatty acid
     esters   T

Propylene glycol monoesters and
     diesters of fat-forming fatty acids   E

Propylene oxide   M

Propyl-p-hydroxy benzoate (or propyl
     paraben)   P

Propyl paraben (or propyl-p-hydroxy
     benzoate)   P

Protease	EN
(Pyridoxine hydrochloride [or Vitamin B 6])	V
Quillaia extract	Z
Radiation. *See* Gamma radiation	
Red Dye No. 2 (amaranth)	C
(Reduced iron [or iron, reduced])	V
Rennet	EN
Riboflavin (or Vitamin B 2)	C, V
(Riboflavin-5-phosphate [or Vitamin B 2])	V
Saffron	C
Saponin	Z
Saunders wood	C
Shellac	G
Silicon dioxide	A
Silver metal	C
Sodium acetate	pH, M
Sodium acid pyrophosphate	T, pH, S
Sodium acid tartrate	pH
Sodium alginate	T
Sodium aluminum phosphate	T, pH
Sodium aluminum silicate	A
Sodium aluminum sulphate	X, Z, pH
Sodium ascorbate	P
Sodium benzoate	P
Sodium bicarbonate (or bicarbonate of soda)	Z, pH, M

Sodium bisulphate	pH
Sodium bisulphite	P
Sodium carbonate	Z, pH, M
Sodium carboxymethyl cellulose	T
Sodium carrageenan	T
Sodium cellulose glycolate	T
Sodium chlorite	M
Sodium citrate	T, Z, pH, S
Sodium diacetate	P
Sodium dithionite	P
Sodium erythorbate (or sodium isoascorbate)	P
Sodium ferrocyanide decahydrate	A, Z
Sodium fumarate	pH
Sodium furcelleran	T
Sodium gluconate	T, pH
Sodium hexametaphosphate	T, Z, pH, S
Sodium hydroxide	pH, M
Sodium hypochlorite	M
Sodium iso-ascorbate (or sodium erythorbate)	P
Sodium lactate	pH
Sodium lauryl sulphate	Z
Sodium metabisulphite	P
Sodium methyl sulphate	Z
Sodium nitrate	P
Sodium nitrite	P
Sodium phosphate dibasic (or disodium phosphate)	T, Z, pH, S
Sodium phosphate monobasic (or sodium phosphate)	T, pH, S

Sodium phosphate tribasic (or trisodium phosphate)	T, pH
Sodium potassium tartrate	T, pH
Sodium propionate	P
Sodium pyrophosphate tetrabasic	T, pH, S
Sodium salt of methyl-p-hydroxy benzoic acid	P
Sodium salt of propyl-p-hydroxy benzoic acid	P
Sodium silicate	Z
Sodium sorbate	P
Sodium stearate	Z
Sodium stearyl fumarate	B
Sodium stearoyl-2-lactylate	B, T, Z
Sodium sulphate	Z, Y
Sodium sulphite	B, Z, P
Sodium tartrate	T
Sodium thiosulphate	Z
Sodium trimetaphosphate	M
Sodium tripolyphosphate	Z, pH, S, M
Sorbic acid	P
Sorbitan monostearate	T
Sorbitan tristearate	T
Sorbitol	Z
Spermaceti wax	G
Stannous chloride	Z
Stearic acid	Z
Stearyl citrate	S
Stearyl monoglyceridyl citrate	T
Succinnic anhydride	M
Sucrose acetate isobutyrate (or SAIB)	Z

Sulphur dioxide	P
Sulphuric acid	pH, M
Sulphurous acid	P
Sunset yellow FCF	C
Tannic acid	T, Z, FE
Tartaric acid	pH, P
Tartrazine (U.S. Yellow Dye No. 5)	C
(Thiamine hydrochloride [or Vitamin B 1])	V
(Thiamine mononitrate [or Vitamin B 1])	V
(Threonine)	V
Titanium dioxide	C
Tocopherols	P, V
(Tocopherol acetate [or Vitamin E])	V
Tragacanth gum	T
Triacetin (glyceryl triacetate)	Z, E
Tributyrin (glyceryl tributyrate)	E
Tricalcium phosphate (or calcium phosphate tribasic)	A, T, Z, pH, S
Triethyl citrate	T, E
Trisodium phosphate (or sodium phosphate tribasic)	T, pH
(Tryptophane)	V
Turmeric	C
Urea	Y
(Valine)	V
Vegetable oils containing tocopherols	P
(Vitamin A)	V

(Vitamin A acetate)	V
(Vitamin A palmitate)	V
(Vitamin B 1 [or thiamine hydrochloride, thiamine mononitrate])	V
(Vitamin B 2 [or riboflavin, riboflavin-5-phosphate])	V
(Vitamin B 6 [pyridoxine hydrochloride])	V
(Vitamin B 12 [cyanocobalamin])	V
(Vitamin D 2)	V
(Vitamin D3)	V
(Vitamin E [tocopherols, tocopherol acetate])	V
(Vitamin K)	V
Wood smoke	P
Xanthan gum	T
Xanthophyll	C
Xylitol	Z
Yellow Dye No. 5 (tartrazine)	C
Zein	G
Zinc sulphate	Y

About Pollution Probe

Pollution Probe, founded in 1969, is an independent registered charitable foundation and one of Canada's leading public interest groups. Probe has been at the forefront of many of Canada's central environmental issues for over a decade. The organization has been responsible for significant steps forward in alleviating air and water pollution, curbing the generating of solid waste, promoting recycling, adopting better land use policies and implementing stricter control on toxic chemicals in our environment.

Projects of the Foundation are the Pollution Probe research team, Ecology House (12 Madison Avenue, Toronto, Ontario, an urban demonstration of conservation in the home) and the *Probe Post* (a bimonthly newspaper).

This book was written as part of Pollution Probe's ongoing work in the area of human exposure to potentially harmful substances.

For more information on Probe, write to:

Pollution Probe
University of Toronto
Toronto, Ontario
M5S 1A1